Naked and Transparent

Six Vital Tools
for Knowing Yourself
and Attracting
Healthy Relationships

Naked and Transparent

Six Vital Tools
for Knowing Yourself
and Attracting
Healthy Relationships

Vladimire Calixte

Fresh Ink Group
Guntersville

Naked and Transparent:
Six Vital Tools for Knowing Yourself and Attracting Healthy Relationships

Fresh Ink Group
An Imprint of:
The Fresh Ink Group, LLC
Box 931
Guntersville, AL 35976
Email: info@FreshInkGroup.com
FreshInkGroup.com

Edition 1.0   2015
Edition 2.0   2018

Cover design by Allison Denise
Book design by Fresh Ink Group

BISAC Subject Headings:
SEL027000   **SELF-HELP / Personal Growth / Success**
OCC019000   **BODY, MIND & SPIRIT / Inspiration & Personal Growth**
FAM030000   **FAMILY & RELATIONSHIPS / Marriage & Long-Term Relationships**

Library of Congress Control Number: 2018948392

ISBN-13: 978-1-947867-11-6 Papercover
ISBN-13: 978-1-947867-12-3 Hardcover
ISBN-13: 978-1-947867-13-0 Ebooks

Naked and TRANSPARENT

SIX VITAL TOOLS FOR KNOWING YOURSELF AND ATTRACTING HEALTHY RELATIONSHIPS

Table of Contents

Foreword

Are you truly happy with who you really are? Are you living a blissful, authentic life that you're proud of? Are you happy in your relationships? If you've answered no to any of these questions, you are about to embark on a powerful new journey that will awaken your heart and soul, and help you create a new beginning.

Becoming self-aware is one of the greatest gifts you can give yourself. If you aren't self-aware, you are doing things that sabotage your relationships, career, happiness, and self-worth.

Many of us are unconsciously holding on to old pain, insecurities, and false beliefs that cause us to create a false self. We may feel that the false self we show the world is more desirable than who we really are and that it protects us from being hurt, but it actually causes us to attract unhealthy partners, accept positions and careers that make us unhappy, and stops us from being truly accepted and loved by others.

Although we are often taught to look outside of ourselves for answers, we are the only ones who can truly save ourselves. It is only through self-awareness that we can truly live the lives we deserve.

It all begins with accepting and loving the person we see in the mirror. Reading this book will help you do just that. It will also help you unlock your deepest fears and release the toxic emotions and behaviors that have been controlling your life and wounding your soul. An accomplished self-help leader, Vladimire Calixte is one of the most revered and highly sought-after mental health specialists and relationship experts of our time.

I've had the pleasure of knowing Vladimire personally, and can say with extreme confidence that she is one of the most compassionate and caring individuals I have ever known. One of Vladimire's many gifts is the ability to empathize with others and anticipate their unmet needs. She is non-judgmental and supportive, and possesses the rare ability to connect with people's hearts and souls easily. People from all walks of life, including celebrities, trust Vladimire whole-heartedly with their most painful secrets, and feel totally safe and loved in her presence.

Vladimire's loving spirit, magnetic personality, resilience, and courage transform the lives of those around her and millions of people around the world. She offers hope to those who need healing in their lives, and is the epitome of conscious living and self-love.

Her infectious words, exceptional wisdom, and provocative teachings truly make the world a better place. Vladimire is a nationally respected expert on mental health, self-esteem, abuse, addiction, and relationships. She is also the founder of Life Rebuilding in New York. For over a decade, Vladimire has been showing individuals, couples, and families how to thrive after trauma, dysfunction, abuse, and addiction. She has also been a valuable resource to the media. She has been featured in *Ebony Magazine* and has appeared on ABC's *Here and Now,* Hot 97 *Street Soldiers with Lisa Evers, Café Mocha* with MC Lyte, Loni Love, and Angelique Perrin, and heard on Fox News Radio and CBS Radio, among others.

Her exciting new book, *Naked and Transparent: Six Vital Tools for Knowing Yourself and Attracting Healthy Relationships,* is an empowering guide that will offer you essential tools to discovering and loving your authentic self, which is the foundation to living an extraordinary, empowered life.

May you find happiness, success, love, and joy!

Florence Edwards, M.A.
CEO of Publicity 911
Los Angeles, California, 2014

Acknowledgments

I would like to thank my Lord and Savior, Jesus Christ. All glory and praise be to you, Heavenly Father.

I thank my wonderful and supportive husband, Alexander Benjamin. You are truly my gift from GOD, and I thank you so much for taking very good care of my heart and our two beautiful children, Tsai-Ann and Isaiah. I love you so much. You are truly the bone of my bone and the flesh of my flesh. You are my love, my anchor, and my best friend.

To my children, Tsai-Ann and Isaiah: I love being your mommy, and you are my two treasures. I promise never to take you both for granted. I love you both deeply, and I am so blessed to have the two of you in my life.

To my mom, Soeurette St. Preux: You sacrificed so much as a single mother of two young girls. Upon migrating to the United States from Haiti, you were determined to make a better life for us. I truly admire your courage and resilience. I love you, Mom!

To Guillermo Calixte and Paulette Calixte: In-laws like you are the best gift ever to me. Guillermo Calixte: You are my gift from heaven. Paulette Calixte: You've both helped me through many trials and tribulations. I thank you both for always being there and showing me you truly care.

To Florence Edwards and Charla Mackey of Publicity 911: I am humbled by your faith in me from the beginning. I thank you so much for always treating me as your only client amongst your many. You have helped me make my dreams come to fruition. For that, I am truly grateful.

To Kirk Watari of Best Web Choice: You were with me from the beginning. From the bottom of my heart I thank you for your time, diligence, and patience.

To Donna Erickson of A Flair For Writing; Charles Davis of Davis Images; Lenny Cavallaro, my editor; and proofreader Amy Thompson of Amy Thompson Editing: It has been an absolute pleasure working with you. I have learned so much from you. You took care of this book as though it were your own from start to finish. I thank you so kindly for helping me piece everything together. This book is very dear to my heart, and you have made it come to life.

Thanks to my publisher, Fresh Ink Group. You came at such an important time in my life, a time of renewal and transformation. You make a really good team. I look forward to working with you to publish many more books.

To my family and friends: I thank you for your love and unending support and encouragement. I feel so blessed to have you all in my life. Thank you for being there and I love each and every one of you tremendously. I could not have written this book on my own.

I stand on the shoulders of: Myriam St. Preux, Marie Paulette Rene, Marie Chantal Rene, Constance Cange, Barbara Cange Dameus, Patrick Calixte, Guillermo, Jr. Calixte, Laeticia Landais, Marie Claude Albert, Shilda Albert, Louise Albert, Carline Marcelin, Marie Evangeline Roussel, Myrtho Cherichel, Barbara Roussel, Samara Jean-Baptiste, Lucy Doutache, Raymonde Jean-Baptiste, Lucinda Jean-Baptiste, Roland Cherasard, Gary Jean-Enard, Wilson Rene, Tamara Rene-Nelson, Nesta Findlay-Givhans, Carlene Burke, Bree and Steven Pascal, Malikah and Andre Johnson, Sadie and Brad Lanzet, Pauline Hospidales, Maria Montes, Angela McGuire, Marcia Cyrus, Nelson Santoni Jr, Ayleen Alago, Harriet Safran, Pat Wright, Joe Turner, Beverly Middleton, Michelle and George Louis-Jeune, Tracy Calixte, Liza H. Herzberg, Jennifer Nelson, Kadmiel Valcin, Jeniece Nimmons-Drake, Alacia Davis, John Nardozzi, Annie Jennings PR, Lila Green, Angela Hadl, MarcArthur St Juste, Aisha Goodridge, Nancy Francois, and Claire Marie Sejour.

In cherished memory of my grandmother, Esperanta Rene; my grandfather, Raphael St. Preux; and my cousin, Andre S. Albert. Time goes on, and the days pass by; however, my memories of you will never die.

Naked and Transparent:

Six Vital Tools for Knowing Yourself and Attracting Healthy Relationships

"I choose not to blame myself. I release my instinctive emotional response from the deepest root cause, and free myself from shame and self-judgment." (Author Unknown)

Introduction

Are you struggling in your relationships? Do you suffer from low self-worth, chronic fear, anxiety, shame, or fear of abandonment? Are you continually attracting abusive partners and toxic relationships that don't honor you, even though you say you want to attract healthy relationships?

If you've answered "yes" to any of these questions, I'm excited to tell you there's hope and that you will create a much juicier and fulfilling life than you've ever dreamed possible! Regardless of where you are in your life right now, increased self-awareness will create miracles and help you achieve phenomenal success in your relationships.

Healthy, long-term relationships require two whole human beings who accept and love themselves, flaws and all. If you truly want to change your life and are ready to do the work to heal thoughts, beliefs, and behaviors that are keeping you from having what you want and being who you really are, you'll no longer be locked and bound in your pain and the fear that holds you back in your life.

The book you now hold in your hands is a powerful and unique guide that will give you some of the most important tools you need to help you break through self-defeating habits and attract your ideal life and relationships. Since you're reading this book, I am convinced that you are committed to becoming more self-aware and empowered.

The path towards self-awareness will be challenging, but I will be here for you every step of the way to support you in your journey. I want to thank you for inviting me into your home and into your heart, and for allowing me to help you excel in your life.

My deep passion for living life exactly as we were meant to be is what led me to working in the mental health field. As a therapist, my mission is to facilitate your transformation—that internal point of change at which you begin to think about your life in a brand new way and become aware of what's truly possible for you. You begin to celebrate, embrace, and honor who you are.

In order to do that, you have to become clear about who you really are, and who you are not. The continuous journey of knowing yourself takes extreme courage, but once you embark on it, you release yourself from the prison of fear, hopelessness, and failed relationships. The one thing that we all have in common—the one thing we all want more than anything else—is to be whole and to live in our own truth.

This book will challenge you to look inside your soul and get to know the real you. You will begin to make new choices based on the real you, and these will change your life. The purpose of this book is to serve as a catalyst for self-knowledge and self-awareness by having you whole-heartedly examine what you want, uncover your unmet needs and beliefs, and discover who you really are.

I am a big proponent of the old adage that when you come to know who you really are, it will change the way you live as well as the way you love. Furthermore, when you come to know yourself and work towards self-mastery and understanding, you will gain an unparalleled sense of clarity. This clarity will then help you establish responsibility for your life and your choices.

My goal in writing this book is to challenge the way you think about your past—your successes, failures, life choices, and relationships—in order to help you grow and ultimately accept your true self. We often want other people to love us unconditionally, but we do not love ourselves unconditionally and have a non-existent relationship with ourselves.

We often put up an emotional wall that distances us, not only from others, but from ourselves as well. If we are not connected with ourselves, it is almost impossible to attract what we want. What do you deeply desire? Is it love? Money? Success? Regardless of what you want, I have come to the understanding that self-awareness is the foundation for receiving it and experiencing lasting joy.

Let me ask you a question: Who do you think you *really* are? I am challenging you to be truthful about who you think you are, because when you are truthful with yourself, you will be truthful about your relationships, goals, and dreams.

Self-awareness allows you to gain greater insight into yourself as an individual and your relationships. It will help you become consistently willing to attend to yourself and your relationships consciously.

Please note that not knowing who you really are doesn't make you a failure. If you feel shame from not knowing yourself, congratulate yourself on embarking down the path of self-discovery. The fact that you have a desire to know yourself is a huge step in achieving what you want.

If you read the book in its entirety and complete your assignments, I promise that you will see tremendous changes in every aspect of your life! You will feel more happiness, more confidence, and more peace than you've experienced before! I know, because I was once in your shoes and used the very techniques I have described in this book to become who I am today.

You can't change something until you are aware of it, and my job is to help you uncover the truth. I highly recommend that you take the time to be unwaveringly honest with yourself. The path of ruthless, honest truth may be uncomfortable and/or downright unpleasant, but neither is it pleasant to live day after day, year after year, pretending to be someone you aren't.

Regardless of the past, this book is all about the here and now. Although I do encourage you to delve into your past in order to pinpoint or locate the source of your primary wound, the goal is for you to become aware of how your beliefs and feelings are serving you now. As we work together to uncover your true self, I challenge you to do so without self-judgment.

We all have parts of us that are healthy and positive, as well as some parts that need improvement. Self-awareness allows you to see aspects of your personality and behavior you didn't notice before. It is not an invitation, however, for you to be hard on yourself. Instead of judging yourself or engaging in negative self-talk, encourage yourself to continue on your path, and know that you truly are worthy and lovable as you are in this very moment. Here's something to think about:

> *There is tremendous power in knowing yourself and allowing that understanding to help guide your life.*

This book will get you from where you are to where you want to be, which requires you to work at developing your self-awareness.

Here are some key points to think about as you read this book:

- You must first take charge of yourself and decide that you are capable of doing, being, and acting differently. You have to decide it's up to you and not pass along your personal power to others.

- If you are looking for a quick fix, this book is not for you. Quick fixes do not work when deep emotional pain is present. True healing, which is not instantaneous, must take place in order for you to experience lasting changes in your life. This book is about your journey, and will serve as a guide to acquiring true self-knowledge.

- Moments of true self-realization can offer a surprising release from years of self-doubt, fear, and shame. Self-awareness transforms the soul and heals the heart.

- This book is meant to be interactive, and it highly promotes self-reflection and realization. Although self-actualization doesn't happen overnight, this book will help you develop a deeper sense of self over time once you surrender and listen to your own heart.

Although therapists are thought to "have it all together," we are not impervious to life's issues. In this book, I felt strongly compelled to share with you some of my past experiences, which have shaped me into the woman I am today. Like many young girls growing up, I longed for my father. I had a mother who loved me, but I felt an emptiness deep inside because my father wasn't in my life. My pain almost tore me apart, but when I learned who I was and took back my power, my life was never the same. Throughout the book, I have incorporated some of the letters that I wrote to my father during my journey from deep pain to inner peace.

These very personal letters were my emotional cleansing tools. My ultimate desire in sharing them with you is as follows: As a therapist, I assist people in having the courage to be real. As such, a therapist must also demonstrate that same courage.

My letters to my father demonstrate my journey to self-acceptance and self-awareness by having the courage to admit my own vulnerability. Furthermore, it is important for me to model genuineness by disclosing my past fears. My mom did her very best as a single mother; however, my father's absence was very painful to me for a long time.

Living that experience was a source of hurt and anger, and I suffered from feelings of diminishment.

I understand "emptiness" and "worthlessness," because at the time, I thought that maybe I was not good enough for my father to stay around. When I came to realize through self-awareness that he *chose* not to be around, I was then able to journey from deep emotional pain to inner serenity.

This is my truth, and I share it with you wholeheartedly; it is uncensored, naked, and transparent. These letters are my way of giving myself permission to be truly honest and transparent with you.

How to Use This Book

Throughout this book, you will find various exercises and fills-ins. Don't try to answer these questions in your head, as it doesn't work. Something special happens when you put pen to paper. It increases your attention span and ability to focus, and easily tracks your thoughts. A very crucial part of knowing yourself is writing about your innermost feelings. Therefore, it is extremely important for me to present this book as part workbook, part self-help guide.

I find that journaling is a powerful way to excavate the significance of your own stories and experiences, and it is a very effective way to coax out thoughts, questions, and insights into your patterns of behavior.

> *"The nicest part is being able to write down all my thoughts and feelings; otherwise, I might suffocate."*
>
> ~ *Anne Frank*

As you engage in the special exercises in the book, I would like you to write as much as you want and whatever comes to mind. There are no right or wrong answers. If a question makes you feel uncomfortable or unpleasant, I would like you to think about why, and I encourage you to complete the exercises regardless of your apprehension. I find the thoughts or feelings that make us feel the most vulnerable are usually what will help us grow the most.

The exercises I present will challenge you to take a personal inventory of yourself and your life. They involve a ruthlessly honest and, at times, not so pretty look at our true selves and needs, which will ultimately help us to tap into our personal power.

One of the most important things you can do to get to know yourself and your true feelings is to make a note of what it feels like when you write down your responses. Observe your thoughts and stay with the feelings, whether they're good or bad. Radical self-honesty really can work miracles, and you will begin to see that as you complete these exercises.

Ultimately, for this book to serve its purpose, you are going to have to be completely honest with yourself: no pretense and no mask. I would like you to think about what *you* really want to get out of this experience, not what your partner, your family member, or anyone else wants.

In the forefront of your mind, you should consider the following questions:

What do I want to get out of reading and engaging in this book? (2) What do I need in order to get what I truly want? (3) What can I do to help myself get what I want? And (4) Am I being honest with myself?

Self-knowledge is essential in figuring out what is optional and what is necessary for our individual well-being. Knowing what you need and responding to that need is the key. Real power comes from authenticity and self-awareness.

Before you begin reading this book, I would also like to talk to you about your inner critic. Yes, I mean that overly harsh voice in your head. At times, our quest for personal growth can get distorted and end up creating self-judgments and self-criticisms. For the purpose of getting the most out of this book, I challenge you to take a moment to think about the following:

1. Recognize how you communicate to yourself.
2. Identify the circumstances under which your inner critic tends to show up more.
3. Understand that your inner critic will judge you, no matter what.
4. Notice what you criticize yourself the most for.

I criticize myself the most for: _____

_____

_____

_____

_____

_____

I've noticed that I tend to beat myself up when:

_____

_____

_____

_____

_____

_____

5. Identify who is speaking. Is it your inner critic or is it realistic thinking?

   Listen to the tone of the words that you hear in your head. The inner critic will sound anxious, fearful, nervous, non-specific, and general. It will say things like, "You always get this wrong," or "If you end this relationship (although it does not serve you well), you will be all alone."

   It's important to note that the inner critic does not look for or move towards any resolutions for the concerns it is voicing. Your realistic thinking, however, is optimistic, solution-oriented, and emotionally uncharged.

6. Whose voice is it? Is it your parents', your own, or your partner's?

   It is important to note that as harsh as the inner critic can be, it wants to "protect you" and keep you "safe." It is a protective defense mechanism that prevents you from living your truth, and also from becoming your authentic self and living an empowered life.

The danger of listening to the inner critic is that it does not know the future, always lives in the past, and projects assumptions about the future. It keeps us from experiencing and staying in the present moment. Our inner critic knows nothing about self-awareness. I see the inner critic as the antagonist of self-awareness. As such, it is imperative that you consciously decide to take control of the thoughts you have in your head.

When you hear your inner critic, it is important to make a realistic assessment by identifying what is true and what is judgment. From there, you can begin to build a healthier relationship with your inner critic, and a stronger relationship with your true self.

Something to Think About!

"My true relationship is with myself — all others are simply mirrors of it."

- Shakti Gawain

Our friendships and intimate relationships all show us who we really are. They expose us to our true beliefs about ourselves and what we think we deserve. If you say you want a good man/woman but believe in your heart that you are unworthy, you will continually attract partners who mirror your true beliefs, thoughts, and feelings.

If you are abusive to yourself in words, thoughts, and actions, you will attract abusive partners. Many of us claim we seek healthful relationships but find ourselves attracting what we say we don't want. Here's a great example of what I mean.

Nikki has been dating the same man since she was 18. At times, he's tall; at other times, he's short. He sometimes has facial hair, and at other times, he doesn't. The only things that remain fairly consistent are his personality traits. No matter how hard Nikki tries to attract a different type of man, she keeps choosing the same partner with the same dysfunctional character traits.

As such, Nikki's relationships predictably take a similar path. These may be referred to as "revolving relationships" and afflict many of us. Since Nikki chooses not to examine this constant, recurring pattern, she is bound to repeat it. It is important for Nikki to take some time to look at why she chooses these partners, and how her choices lead to disastrous relationships.

First, however, she must be willing to accept and acknowledge the motivations underlying her choices in men. Nikki can start her self-inquiry by asking herself the following:

"Who am I?"

"What types of people do I enjoy spending time with?" "What am I really seeking?"

"Am I afraid to be alone?"

Once she's truthful with herself and sorts out her feelings, she can accept whatever it is she is considering as an evident truth, without judgment.

We inevitably gain self-understanding through our relationships. Whatever the pattern we feel stuck in, we can challenge it and eventually change it by changing our thoughts and beliefs. That's the power of insights and realizations. If you are willing to be self-aware, you can empower yourself and transform your life and relationships in the process.

We must muster the courage to go beyond our pain in order to create a life that brings us lasting joy and satisfaction. We must also make different choices that serve us and our true desires.

Can you relate to Nikki's experience? Have you been dating the same woman or the same man but just with different names? Do you recognize any destructive patterns in your relationships? If so, what are they? How is this pattern or these patterns serving you now?

What kinds of situations seem to trigger these negative behaviors? Can you identify any unmet childhood needs? If so, what are they? Once you examine your choices and why you made them, you can begin to stop the patterns that rob you of your happiness.

Honesty is the path to true self-awareness, but it requires courage to face what you fear or find difficult to accept.

Once you are honest with yourself about what you really want, who you are, and what your real needs are, you will begin to attract more of what you want and less of what you don't want.

However, in order to begin to start knowing yourself, you must first ask one of the most important questions you'll ever ask yourself: Who am I?

Chapter 1

Who Am I? The Power of Clarity

"Only the truth of who you are, if realized, will set you free."

— *Eckhart Tolle*

"It's easy to take off your clothes and have sex; people do it all the time. But opening up your soul to [people], letting them into your spirit, thoughts, fears, future, hopes and dreams … that's being naked."

— *Rob Bell*

When was the last time you were naked in front of someone with your arms flung open, with or without your clothes on? More importantly, when have you been totally naked with yourself? Many of us hide ourselves from the world and from those we say we love. We are also afraid to look at ourselves in the mirror because we fear coming face-to-face with what we truly are.

Do you know who you are? I am not talking about your identity as a father, a mother, a provider, an employee, a friend, a relationship partner, and so on. I am not saying it is wrong to identify with the aforementioned roles.

On the contrary, our connections with others tell us a lot about who we are. However, our roles do not tell the whole story about our real identity. I know this may sound a little confusing, because to some degree, we all get our identity from what we do. This is especially true if one of our roles requires a huge commitment, like being a parent. When you think about it, so many things in life depend on our ability to connect with our true self.

Besides, how are we supposed to know what we should be doing or with whom we should be doing it, if we don't know who we really are? It is important to develop relationships with others, as well as a relationship with our outer selves—and our inner selves—our thoughts, feelings, values, and beliefs. When it is just you, alone in the quiet of total solitude, who are you? Ask yourself, "Who am I?" Pay attention to the thoughts that come into your head.

In the pages that follow, you will go through a series of questions. I am challenging you to be uncommonly honest with yourself. Self-awareness is a two-edged sword, as we might find out something about ourselves we would rather not know. If you indeed find things about yourself you do not like, you must learn to accept them and accept yourself without engaging in self-criticism or negative self-talk.

Self-awareness invites us to find our own inner truth. Our ego has dressed us up for so long that many of us don't even know how to begin to peel back the layers to get to the naked truth about ourselves. It takes courage to make a decision to be transparent. Most of us have been acting out the role and living up to the identity we have given ourselves. However, we are so much more than we think we are.

Stripped naked, who are you at your core? Is there a disconnection between what people see and who you really are? Have you ever felt no one knows who you really are? The transformative process of exploring your core identity and answering the question—"Who am I?"—will take you on a journey through your inner feelings, thoughts, and beliefs, and help you look at your relationships and the roles you play.

When we have self-awareness, we also have a concrete understanding of who we really are—our essence and true nature! A good understanding of your true identity does not mean being the way we wish we were, or think we ought to be, or what others think we should be.

Once you are fully invested in that pursuit, you may even get a glimpse of what your true purpose in life is. This is the beginning of an ongoing process.

The questions I present to you throughout this book may feel uncomfortable at times. However, simply completing them can be a healing experience in itself. Part of self-exploration involves recognition of what one feels. The drills in this section will help you to begin to get to know yourself better. Your responses will help reveal your truth.

1. Think back to when you were about twelve years old. How would someone who knew you at that age have described you?

_____

_____

_____

_____

_____

_____

_____

2. Think of three things about yourself NOW that answer the question, "Who am I?" Please note that your answers cannot refer to your identity as a mother, father, husband, lover, sister, friend, employee, etc. Think about qualities and/or characteristics you have.

_____

_____

_____

_____

_____

_____

_____

_____

_____

3. I asked you to name three words that describe who you are. These can be your qualities, feelings, or beliefs. For example, a quality might be, "I am trustworthy." A feeling might be, "I feel angry." A belief might be, "I believe loyalty is important." Try to write fifteen sentences that describe your thoughts, feelings, beliefs, and qualities. These words will help you describe your inner self.

1. _____

2. _____

3. _____

4. _____

5. _____

6. _____

7. _____

8. _____

9. _____

10. _____

11. _____

12. _____

13. _____

14. _____

15. _____

How did it feel to respond to these questions? We are about to delve deeper, as I challenge you to take a brave look at your life in the present moment. My hope is that the questions below will provide you with an opportunity to get acquainted with your natural, authentic self. Take an utterly honest inventory of your life as you answer.

1. What do you feel strongly about? What are your core beliefs?

_____

_____

_____

_____

_____

_____

2. What do you want more than anything in your life?

_____

_____

_____

_____

_____

_____

_____

3. What things from your past are influencing you right now?

_____

_____

_____

_____

_____

_____

_____

_____

4. What thoughts or behaviors have you picked up in your life that serve as a liability rather than an asset?

_____

_____

_____

_____

_____

_____

_____

5. What fear or shame to which you are holding on is not allowing your life to work at this time?

_____

_____

_____

_____

_____

_____

_____

6. Are you proud of the way you have been living your life? Why or why not?

_____

_____

_____

_____

_____

_____

_____

_____

7. What is your greatest personal achievement?

_____

_____

_____

_____

_____

_____

_____

_____

8. What gives your life joy and fulfillment, either personally or professionally?

   _____

   _____

   _____

   _____

   _____

   _____

   _____

   _____

9. What are some of the things you are obstinately holding on to or wearing as an armor that are causing
   you great pain or stifling your personal growth and
   development?

   _____

   _____

   _____

   _____

   _____

   _____

   _____

10. What should you be doing more of?

_____

_____

_____

_____

_____

_____

_____

_____

_____

11. What should you be doing less of?

_____

_____

_____

_____

_____

_____

_____

_____

_____

12. What is the one deep commitment or value from which you would never waiver?

_____

_____

_____

_____

_____

_____

_____

13. What would you do with your life if you had it to live over?

_____

_____

_____

_____

_____

_____

_____

14. What would your life be like if nothing was holding you back?

_____

_____

_____

_____

_____

_____

_____

_____

15. I am …

_____

_____

_____

_____

_____

_____

_____

_____

_____

16. I hear …

_____

_____

_____

_____

_____

_____

_____

17. I see myself as …

_____

_____

_____

_____

_____

_____

_____

_____

18. My life purpose is …

_____

_____

_____

_____

_____

_____

_____

_____

19. My talents and gifts are …

_____

_____

_____

_____

_____

_____

_____

_____

20. I am going to decide to do_____, no matter what.

_____

_____

_____

_____

_____

_____

_____

_____

21. I am true to myself in the following situations …

_____

_____

_____

_____

_____

_____

_____

_____

22. In what situations am I not true to myself?

_____

_____

_____

_____

_____

_____

_____

_____

23. What advice would you give to your eighteen-year-old self?

_____

_____

_____

_____

_____

_____

_____

_____

_____

24. I give myself permission to …

_____

_____

_____

_____

_____

_____

_____

_____

25. My ideal life looks like …

_____

_____

_____

_____

_____

_____

_____

_____

_____

26. What I really want is …

_____

_____

_____

_____

_____

_____

_____

_____

27. I am not honest with myself when it comes to …

_____

_____

_____

_____

_____

_____

_____

_____

28. I am radically honest with myself when it comes
to ...

_____

_____

_____

_____

_____

_____

_____

29. I am in active pursuit of ...

_____

_____

_____

_____

_____

_____

_____

_____

30. At the end of this year, what one accomplishment would bring your life the greatest joy and satisfaction?

_____

_____

_____

_____

_____

_____

_____

_____

With self-awareness comes a paradigm shift in thinking. When you start to look deep inside yourself and begin your personal journey to authenticity, you will find the following:

- As you gain a better understanding of who you really are, you will communicate better.
- Self-awareness will greatly diminish miscommunication. With greater self-awareness comes an increase in honest communication, so you can better express your feelings.
- Awareness will enable you to understand your emotions and why you feel the way you do, thus allowing

you to act responsibly on those feelings. Think about how much happier you would be in your relationships, but most importantly with yourself, if you engaged in authentic and direct communication. Self-awareness allows us to demonstrate frankness, candor, and honest, direct communication.

- Without being self-aware, how can you be authentic? How can you have the courage to be yourself, if you do not know what it means to be yourself? Only when you come to knowing who you are—your core values, emotions, and idiosyncrasies—can you live your truth.

- When you know who you are, you will know how to position yourself to receive the direction for your life's journey.

- When you come to know who you really are, you become aware of your strengths and limitations.

- Do you know who the "real you" is, and if so, do you let him or her out regularly?

- Two of the most important things you will ever do on your way to personal power are to learn who you really are and to define your essence.

- As painful as it may be, once you start to tear away at the wrapping, you will find a very powerful you inside. The real person will be empowered, because you'll no longer need to impress others or lie to yourself.

- Self-awareness puts us on the path to finding out our soul's agenda.

- When you know who you are, you will know what kind of romantic relationships to get involved in and which ones to stay far away from. You will understand who is or is not a good fit for you, and how the relationship relates to your joy and happiness.

- Furthermore, you will realize that when you engage with the wrong people, it will have an adverse affect on your life. You will come to know unequivocally whom to surround yourself with.

- Self-awareness is important in every area of your life, and it's essential when dealing with relationships. If you're aware of the things you say and do, you'll be able to recognize the way your actions affect others.

- You will consciously present your thoughts, emotions, actions, and intentions.

- If you are having some difficulty with the question, "who am I?" how about starting with the opposite: "Who am I not?" To know who you truly are, you have to recognize who you are not. Most times, the pain is so deep we don't realize we already know the answers.

- For example, what are some things you would NOT compromise, regardless of anything? By digging deep down to respond to this, you will begin to know who you are not. You will start to see your greatness, your abilities, and all of the potential you have on the inside of you.

- By the way, greatness is in your DNA. Your greatness is inevitable! Self-awareness allows you to tap into your greatness. Wrapped up in you is your vision and purpose. However, in order to discover that vision and purpose, you have to have a clear understanding of who you are.

- The world is full of doubters and naysayers who are ready to define you at the drop of a dime. But what do you believe? How do you define yourself?

- Self-awareness leads you to your innate strengths. How can you discover something when you are not aware of it?

- When you know who you are, you make better decisions and life choices, as you will know what is optional and what is not optional to your overall individual wellbeing.

- When you know who you really are, you no longer have the need to convince others of your worth by being subservient or manipulative. Thus, there is no need for a demonstration or a spotlight, because you are living from within.

So many of us are doing what everyone else tells us to do, we get so caught up in pleasing others, that we completely forget to be who we are. I know this feeling too well, since I was in that same situation years ago.

After college, I entered the nursing program at NYU. However, I realized two semesters into the program that nursing was not for me, as I was terrified of blood. I took six months off to reassess what I wanted to do, deciding on the rehabilitation counseling program, where I earned a master's degree in applied psychology.

This was a time of great distress for me, as I was still in the people-pleasing stage. For most of my life, I had been doing what I thought others wanted me to do.

During my time of reassessment and self-reflection, I began to see that I hadn't tried to become a nurse because it was my passion, rather, because my mom is a nurse, and I so desperately wanted to please her at the time.

For my overall wellbeing, I had to make my life decisions based on who I am as well as who I am not. Believe it or not, I used these same, exact questions I used in this book to assess and evaluate who I really was. I am not saying it was easy, and in fact it was painful when I started to peel back the layers to get to my truth.

However, it would have been even more painful to live my life pretending. Life, as it progresses, has a way of showing us what we're made of. I realized I was working harder at pleasing other people but ignoring the inner me.

I have always had a very strong passion to help people and have always felt a connection with people in a variety of different ways. From a very young age, I was concerned about other people, particularly in terms of how they were feeling. People would confide their innermost thoughts with me, as they trusted me. Additionally, they sought advice from me. I have always been told that I am non-judgmental and accept people for who they are. As such, a career in therapy was a natural fit, as it enabled me to help people on a greater scale and help them make better life choices. I have been excited and fulfilled ever since I began to listen to my own heart and follow my own bliss.

Although it takes courage to follow your own dreams and be true to yourself, the challenge will make you a stronger, wiser, and happier person. If I had not listened to my inner voice, I would not be where I am today. The struggle was worth it. It takes courage to decide not to hide, but to live, and to live life on your own terms.

Can you relate to my past experience? Can you pinpoint a time in your life where you were working harder on something other than living your truth?

I would like you to write down eight things that would bring you a feeling of tremendous satisfaction if you had the courage to do them.

1. _____

2. _____

3. _____

4. _____

5. _____

6. _____

7. _____

8. _____

What, if added to your life, would make you happier?

_____

_____

_____

_____

_____

_____

_____

_____

_____

What in life already makes you happy?

_____

_____

_____

_____

_____

_____

_____

_____

_____

In what aspect of your life do you already feel successful?

_____

_____

_____

_____

_____

_____

_____

_____

_____

What do you resent the most frequently in your life?

_____

_____

_____

_____

_____

_____

_____

_____

What's most likely to put you in a bad mood? Why?

_____

_____

_____

_____

_____

_____

_____

_____

Do you find yourself feeling annoyed or jealous of something that someone else is doing? Why?

_____

_____

_____

_____

_____

_____

_____

_____

_____

Chapter 2

Letting Go of Your Shame

Shame involves a sense of *being wrong*, which means you feel something is intrinsically "bad" about you, and it is not easily remedied. Real shame is not as much about the deed you committed, as about thinking something internal must have caused you to commit such a shameful act. This deep feeling causes you to feel unworthy and undeserving of success or happiness.

First, I'll share what Brené Brown has taught me. In her research, she discovered that at the heart of shame is the fear of disconnection. One may ask: If I share something that is not so desirable about myself, will I still be loved and accepted?

Shame keeps us in a place we don't need to be. However, in order to feel *connected*, we have to allow ourselves to be seen; i.e., to be naked and transparent. I know that isn't as easy as it sounds. However, when you live an authentic life and are true to your values, you are less likely to feel shame. I had to look my shame directly in the face.

When I mustered the courage not only to explore the source of my shame but also to share my shame, deep healing began. Shame no longer controlled me; I controlled it! Thus, I reclaimed my power. In dealing with my shame about my father's absence, I realized the more I shared my pain, the more connected I felt to others. Therein lies the paradox. The only way to release my pain was to share my truth about my father's absence.

I can remember the first time I told my story to a trusted friend. I made no omissions and quickly started to feel better. The more I shared my truth, the more I began to release my shame. I am encouraging you to let it out! In order to heal and to be free, you have to articulate your shame. There is great value in you. As such, there is also great value in your story, no matter what circumstance you may find yourself in at the present moment.

As you read the following statements, I would like you to be fully aware of your responses.

I feel or felt deep shame about:

_____

_____

_____

_____

_____

_____

_____

_____

_____

_____

_____

_____

_____

_____

_____

I first started to feel this shame when:

_____

_____

_____

_____

_____

_____

_____

_____

_____

_____

_____

_____

_____

_____

_____

_____

I have been perpetuating this shame by:

_____

_____

_____

_____

_____

_____

_____

_____

_____

_____

_____

_____

_____

_____

_____

_____

I overcame this shame by:

_____

_____

_____

_____

_____

_____

_____

_____

_____

_____

_____

_____

_____

_____

Finally, I would like you to visualize the following: Picture me holding a clean, crisp $100 bill in my hand. Now visualize me handing this brand new $100 bill to you. You crumple it up, drop it on the ground, and start to grind it into the floor with your shoe. You pick it up, and it is now wrinkled and dirty.

My question to you is whether this $100 bill still has its value?

No matter what you did to the money, you still want it, because it did not decrease in value. It is still worth $100. Many times in our lives we are dropped, crumpled, beaten, and ground into the dirt by either the decisions we have made or the circumstances that have come our way.

Due to the negative experiences we faced in our lives, we feel as though we are worthless. But no matter what has happened or what will happen, you will never lose your value. Dirty or clean, crumpled or finely creased, you are still priceless. You are always worthy, and you deserve great things.

Chapter 3

Putting a Name to Your Wound

Are you allowing your wounds to change who you are and ultimately control your destiny? If so, it's time to write a new story, recasting yourself as someone who has overcome these obstacles!

In order to heal, we must first determine the following: (1) what are we actually feeling and (2) why we are feeling that way. It is truly transformative to identify our wounds. However, we have been conditioned to look as though we are not hurting.

We're often trained to minimize our pain. Well-meaning parents (or some not-so-well-meaning ones) urge us to "stop crying," and tell us that "it's not so bad" and that we should "get over it." As a result, we learn that our tears and indeed our pain itself make others uncomfortable. Consequently, we stop crying and tell ourselves its not so bad, but rarely do we get over it that easily. That's because whatever caused the injury is still there. Untreated, it will simply fester.

Emotional pain can be harder to deal with than physical trauma. This is because there's nothing to point to—no blood and no broken bone. Our emotional distress is invisible to the naked eye.

It's important for us to remember that the past, unless effectively dealt with, is your present. Furthermore, until you recognize that hidden wound, it will emerge in all of your relationships. Thus, you must deal directly with the hurt.

Pinpointing the impairment will provide satisfying relief by acknowledging the depth of what you have been through and to be able move forward. What's more, your response to what happened will begin to make sense. You will no longer think something is wrong with you because you simply cannot "get over it." You will begin to understand that your pain is so deep and so profound that you need self-compassion, not criticism.

There is no "right" way to identify your wound. There is only your own truth. For many of us, emotional wounds left untended, will indeed worsen and continue to contaminate our relationships with others and with ourselves. They will manifest in unhealthy behaviors, such as overeating, sexual or shopping addictions, drug use, and other self-destructive actions.

We must reconsider what is really going on and become more honest about it. When we treat our wounds and our responses to them—fear, rage, shame, and resentment—as foreign bodies that threaten our wellbeing, we become more willing to search deep within ourselves to remove them. It can be terrifying to go to that place where our darkest feelings lie; however, there is no other way forward – at least no other healthy way. And know this: shame and fear are not part of your natural self. I have come to understand that self-awareness is one of the main ingredients to getting back to our natural, authentic selves. Moreover, self-awareness is the greatest enemy of shame.

Take a moment and think about your last physical wound. Did the wound heal? How long did it take to heal? We cannot cure the lesions simply by ignoring the hurt. Without applying the correct treatment, we have little hope for healing and positive, lifelong change.

I believe that no one desires to live with open sores. People yearn for their wounds to heal, but very few are aware of the proper step-by-step procedures that will make this possible. Self-awareness propels us to operate in a state of truth: the truth about who we really are, and the truth about our shame, anger, trauma, doubt, and/or abandonment.

I want to share a quote with you that I came up with when I began writing this book: "Yesterday, you were pregnant with fear; however, today you will give birth to boldness." Tremendous healing power will emerge as you identify your pain. You can start by honestly asking yourself: "What is really bothering me?"

Where do I go from here?

It is important to note that healing your past wounds can take many forms. Those who prefer one-to-one inter-action can engage in individual therapy. You can also join a therapy or support group as there is nothing more liberat-ing and powerful than being with others who share similar stories. Some find comfort and healing in journaling. That is why self-awareness is so important.

You must determine what you need in order to move towards that need.

What hidden issue(s) or wound(s) do you need to identify?

_____

_____

_____

_____

_____

_____

_____

_____

_____

_____

_____

_____

_____

_____

What step(s) have you taken towards applying the correct treatment (i.e., therapy, support groups, journaling, etc.)?

_____

_____

_____

_____

_____

_____

_____

_____

_____

_____

_____

_____

_____

_____

Chapter 4

I Choose Me

As you move through life, there is only one common denominator: you. You have to spend the rest of your life with you. That's why a nurturing, encouraging, loving, and kind relationship with yourself is extremely important. When you truly understand yourself, you cannot help feeling a powerful, unconditional love for yourself. Moreover, when you truly love and know yourself—and the powerful feeling of loving yourself can manifest only when you have come to know yourself—then you can love and understand others. Nothing is more powerful and liberating than becoming in tune with who you are.

Self-awareness allows you to gain greater insight into yourself as an individual and the relationships you form. You become consistently and consciously willing to attend to your relationships with yourself and with others.

When you choose to love yourself, you're affirming your own greatness.

You are saying: "I am lovable. I deserve happiness. I deserve success." If you choose to love yourself, it will be mirrored back to you.

You can begin by simply saying, "I love myself." Say it all the time, especially when you feel least like saying it, and when you feel it's not true or you don't deserve to feel love for yourself. By saying it in those moments, you open up to its possibility. We decide to love ourselves; it's a choice. The decision to love yourself is an extremely profound choice with miraculous and powerful ramifications.

We all desire to be loved and accepted. In doing my own heart work as well as engaging in therapy with my clients, I have come to learn that self-love is the true foundation of lasting joy and fulfillment.

It is about seeking, maintaining, and embracing your truth, and thus remaining true to your "you." Your "you" is your essence. Your "you," which is your true nature, is at the heart of your soul. Self-love must be pursued with an unrelenting passion, as well as an openness to the unexpected. Furthermore, healing cannot occur in the absence of self-love. I have learned and believe wholeheartedly that the starting point for all healing is self-love. We can heal anything in our lives through the power of self-love and self-awareness, and true empowerment comes from looking within and embracing the real you.

Choosing yourself is also about protecting your "you." You may ask, "How do I protect my 'me'?" Just as you can safeguard your home by getting an alarm, you have to safeguard your "you." For instance, not everyone whom you are allowing into your life is good for your "you."

Spend more time with supportive people—people who see the best in you! Spend time each day with people who make you feel good about yourself. It will be hard to keep your self-love up if the most important influences in your life drag it down on a daily basis. The practice of "choosing me" says that you are truly valuing who you are at your core.

"I choose me" can be a difficult concept to grasp, let alone to put into practice. The phrase can conjure up immediate negative reactions, as it appears to be about selfishness. I choose me is quite the contrary. Choosing me is about self-love, self-acceptance, and honoring who you really are, which is the greatest gift we can bring to any relationship. Here's what "choosing me" looks like:

- When we know ourselves, we no longer need to pretend.
- We seek and maintain our truth.
- We can be the best of who we are—not perfect, but perfectly imperfect. Besides, the quest for perfection will lead to the death of the real you.
- I choose me says: "I am unique, and I deserve love."
- I choose me is self-compassionate.
- I choose me means you make time to be alone to think about life.

- I choose me means you accept responsibility for your actions. It's easy to blame our failures or setbacks on other people. We can blame our parents, our spouses, our children, or our co-workers. However, the sooner we realize and accept that we have control of our destinies, the sooner we can take control of changing our lives for the better. We all have experienced discouragement by external forces. Nevertheless, we have to take responsibility for the roles we play.

- I choose me means you are always armed with a positive energy field (PEF). Your PEF is your protective barricade. By putting on your PEF, you are not allowing negativity to toxify your spirit. To reiterate, we have home security systems, car alarms, and computer virus/spyware. Additionally, we take vitamins and eat the right foods to bolster our immune systems. We put on masks and hazardous material suits to protect ourselves from toxins. We wear sunscreens for protection. However, we are lax about protecting our spirits, inner selves, our places of solace. My question to you is: What are you doing to arm and protect your "you"? What are you doing to safeguard your spirit? Thus, the importance of your positive energy field and not allowing yourself to be toxified.

- The positive energy field diagram below illustrates the power we do have over our lives. Ultimately, we control what we let into our lives, and this is our inherent power. I encourage you to study this diagram at length and thereafter ask yourself, "Whom am I giving my power to?"

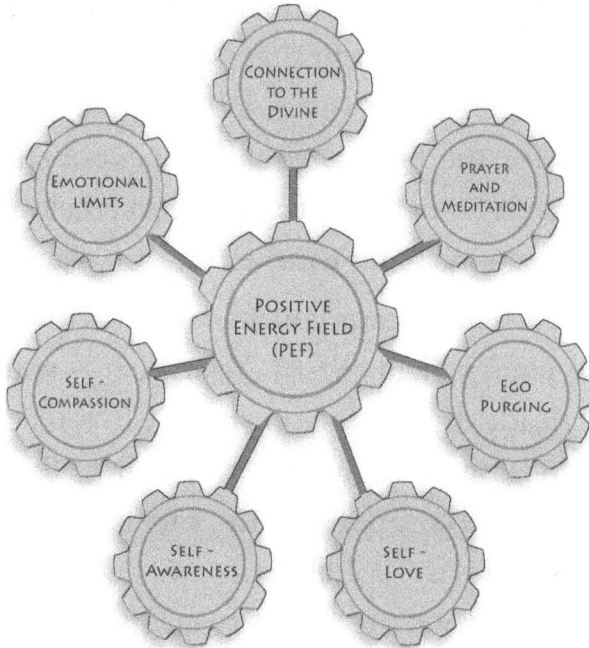

© Copyright March 2015 by Vladimire Calixte

- When you make a commitment to honor yourself (I choose me), you will engage in setting emotional limits, remaining connected to the Divine (through prayer and meditation), and practicing self- awareness, self-compassion, self-love, and ego purging. This will allow your positive energy field to be impenetrable.

- I choose me means you set emotional limits. You no longer compromise your core for the sake of pleasing others. Furthermore, emotional limits allow us to protect ourselves from being manipulated by others.

It is an act of self-love that comes from having a good sense of our own self-worth.

- I choose me means engaging in constant ego purging. Your ego is a part of you, and you can never be rid of it entirely. Nevertheless, you can learn to recognize and overcome it. As such, it is vital for you to observe your thoughts carefully by remaining aware. Ego purging happens when you unequivocally embrace and accept your true self.

- I choose me also means that you accept responsibility for your accomplishments.

- I choose me doesn't mean being self-indulgent or self-ish. I choose me means you are choosing to engage in activities (i.e., self-compassion, self-awareness, etc.) that nourishes your soul.

- I choose me means committing to a plan to move out of stagnation into a life of passion and a sense of purpose.

- I choose me says "No amount of pain from others is worth sacrificing who I am."

- I choose me means you spend time getting to know and like YOU.

- Every time you share or speak your truth, you are protecting your "you" and safeguarding your inner core, that bold and unapologetic expression of who you are.

People want to feel that others understand them, get them, and at the end of it all, love them anyway. Of course, that has to start with ourselves. People can only love us if we believe we're lovable.

Take a moment and step inward. Filter out all the distractions. Stay present with past barriers that may cause hindrance.

Which statement or statements closely reflect what you are feeling?

- — I am constantly compensating for who I am with apologies, hedging words, or clarifications for my actions.
- — I feel as though I always owe other people an explanation.
- — I beat myself up when I make even the slightest mistake.
- — When I think about my flaws, I feel overwhelmingly disgusted or angry.
- — I get overwhelmed with guilt whenever I consider meeting my own needs.
- — I repeatedly do self-destructive things, or make choices that show I don't respect or value myself.
- — It's hard to consider my needs as a priority.
- — What thoughts about yourself have you allowed to creep into your brain, negative thoughts that have

literally taken over, sucking the inner peace, love, and joy out of you?

_____

_____

_____

_____

_____

_____

_____

_____

_____

_____

_____

_____

_____

_____

_____

_____

_____

_____

Whether in the privacy your home or while taking a stroll, I encourage you to repeat the following every day:

Today, I will not allow any negativity to toxify my spirit. I am putting on my positive energy field.

Chapter 5

Getting Comfortable with Vulnerability

"Vulnerability is not weakness. And that myth is profoundly dangerous ... I define vulnerability as emotional risk, exposure, and uncertainty. It fuels our daily lives."

— Dr. Brené Brown

"Vulnerability" immediately conjures up a negative reaction, because most of us have been conditioned to appear as though we are not hurting. We have also been taught that our vulnerability displeases people.

When we look up vulnerable in the dictionary, we find the following synonyms: weak, naked, unsafe, exposed. The antonyms for vulnerable are words associated with safety, strength, and protection.

Vulnerability is a word very few people avoid taking credit for or want to be associated with. Most of us live under the misguided assumption that strong people are those with the ability to control themselves and others. They are typically seen as people who are tough, in control, and nothing ever seems to ruffle them. People who are supposedly "strong" do not show any emotions.

Is this really what we should be calling strength? I don't think that's being strong at all. Bravery is the courage to live from within your soul. The people I consider the most strong are those who are willing not only to process their feelings, but to sit with them long enough to discern what message they can get from these emotions about themselves. They can own their own behaviors, thoughts, and feelings without judgment, and have a clear objective: to see the absolute truth.

The benefits of becoming comfortable with vulnerability are massive. Practicing vulnerability will have a profound impact on everyone you come in contact with, as making yourself vulnerable will draw out not only the best in yourself, but those around you.

Let's think about it for moment. When you make a conscious decision to show your vulnerability, people around you will most likely be more comfortable about showing their vulnerability. As such, vulnerability attracts the right people into our lives, thus creating healthy relationships.

When you make yourself vulnerable, there will be no space for pretension or ambiguity. You are consciously living in a state of perpetual truth and nakedness, a state of perpetual truth while you are aware of the risks, uncertainty, and uncomfortability involved. Now that's conscious and present living.

There's no question that being vulnerable is scary, because it may not be reciprocated. Exposure of any kind is frightening, as we risk rejection, ridicule, or simple misunderstanding. When we make ourselves vulnerable, it is one of the greatest expressions of personal power. We are saying to the world, "This is who I am and how I am choosing to show up in the world." When we practice being vulnerable, we are saying that we are secure and okay with the unexpected.

Most of us associate vulnerability with "weakness" and "softness," but on the contrary, vulnerability embodies strength and courage. It takes courage to make a decision to be naked and transparent in the presence of others. It takes courage to be honest and open about our dreams, fears, expectations, core beliefs, and values.

When we implement vulnerability into our lives, it leads us to direct and honest communication, which in turn, leads to a greater connection and intimacy with those around us. When we choose to practice vulnerability, we are making a conscious decision to live in a state of perpetual risk and are okay with it, because we become aware that we are living in truth—*our* truth.

The lies we tell others and ourselves tell as much about us as the truth. The lie says, "I am afraid. I am afraid people will not like me if I reveal my true self, and that's why I am pretending to be someone else." Vulnerability is about radical self-honesty, which can work miracles.

It is important to note that vulnerability has absolutely nothing to do with gaining the sympathy of another person. If you show vulnerability simply to gain sympathy or love from someone else, you are not being authentic. You are not living your truth. When you show vulnerability, you should not be operating from your ego, as your motive is not out to gain anything from someone else.

There are all kinds of things we call strength that have nothing whatsoever to do with real strength, simply because they are not true. For example, manipulating others or playing the victim role—which gives some people a sense of control in that they can get others to take care of them—is not living in truth. There is no truth in such behaviors. In fact, there is very little life in the aforementioned behaviors.

Implementing vulnerability in our lives is about living from within; building a relationship with your soul. Your vulnerable self is your soul made visible: naked, transparent, and strong. It takes bravery to live within.

When was the last time you felt vulnerable?

_____

_____

_____

_____

_____

_____

_____

_____

_____

_____

_____

_____

_____

What makes you feel vulnerable?

_____

_____

_____

_____

_____

_____

_____

_____

_____

_____

_____

_____

_____

_____

What does vulnerability look like to you?

_____

_____

_____

_____

_____

_____

_____

_____

_____

_____

_____

_____

After you have completed your responses, review them and note what caused you to feel the most vulnerable. Examine the thoughts and feelings that come to your mind. Now, think about how you behave when you feel vulnerable. Do you withdraw, feel anger, become anxious, or lash out? Do you engage in negative self-talk?

The decision to become more vulnerable will require you to let go of past thoughts and behaviors and create new ones. You can begin the process by using some powerful affirmations such as, "I feel safe when I am the real me," or, "I feel good when I express my true feelings." You can also practice being vulnerable by expressing your emotions, or revealing thoughts and fears you have kept hidden with someone you trust.

The more you reveal your truth and you accept yourself as you are, the more comfortable you will feel about being vulnerable. The most important key to becoming more vulnerable is to trust yourself while learning how to be at peace with your perceived flaws. Unconditional love for yourself and increased self-awareness will give you the power to be more vulnerable and have blissful, long-lasting relationships.

Chapter 6

Self-Awareness Puts
a Dim on Introjections

When a new person you encounter mirrors some unresolved issues you had with someone from your past, you may unconsciously attempt to deal with old relationships through your current relationship. This is why it is so important to be self-aware. We are constantly revisiting significant people and family members in our lives. Therefore, it is crucial that you know to whom you are responding: to the individual in front of you, or to a person from your past.

The significant harm found in any wound lies in its ability to change our identities. Many times, the pain changes who we are, and causes us not to know where the wound ends and where we begin. What's more, we accept as introjection an external circumstance, another person's projection, or someone else's personality or emotions. We absorb these things and identify with them so completely that we now see ourselves, at least in part, as that external circumstance or that other person's projection, personality, or emotion.

For example, if someone was sexually abused as a child, he or she might begin to see him/herself as the perpetrator.

One might start to think, "I am guilty, I am bad, and I am despicable." As a result, the person's identity is changed from that of an innocent child to a nasty, evil adult.

In these and other ways, the people introject and change how they see themselves and their lives as a result of the introjection. It is no longer just about the pain of what was done. We change our identities to match the event, person, or circumstance, so that we now become that event, person, or circumstance in some small or large way.

Through the practice of self-awareness, we are able to make the distinction between our true identity and our identification with the introjection. I would like you to stand in front of someone in your current life with whom you are having some difficulty. [1]

This individual (Person 1) might be a spouse, lover, family member, friend, or co-worker. If the person is not present, you can imagine him or her. Take a good look at this person.

Next, let a picture of someone from your past come forward (Person 2). Who comes to mind? How old are you and how old is Person 2? What relationship do you or did you have with this individual you are remembering?

---

[1] Introjection may be defined as the process where the subject replicates in itself behaviors, attributes, or other fragments of the surrounding world, especially of other subjects.

What feelings are linked with this relationship? What did you think about Person 2?

Now, once again, examine your current emotional reactions to Person 1. Do you see any connections or patterns between what Person 1 is evoking in you and the past feelings that Person 2 has evoked?

The aforementioned exercise can help you become aware of the ways in which you are carrying your past into your present interactions. One of the steps to self-awareness is to look at past issues you've had with people and be honest with yourself. Sometimes it's so hard to think we might have messed up that we don't allow ourselves to reflect on the actions we took to help prolong or cause an argument or disagreement.

Admitting you have played a part in how people treat you is a hard concept to embrace at first. With self-knowledge comes acceptance. Once you accept yourself and take responsibility for your actions, you can heal your life and your relationships.

Chapter 7

Letters to My Father

I have asked you to be "naked and transparent." I therefore wanted to be the first partaker. In this chapter, you will find letters I wrote to my father a few years ago, recounting what my life was like in his absence.

After I began learning about myself and getting serious about my wants and needs, I made a conscious decision to locate the source of the original pain that came from my childhood. For me, that initial wound came from my father.

In my passage from pain to inner peace, I decided to write him these letters detailing my experience of living life without him. I decided to write to my father, because I found there could be nothing more powerful than putting my feelings, thoughts, and deep emotional injuries on paper. The following are some of the texts that have helped me heal.

However painful this was for me initially, it was necessary to begin my path to healing. It is important to note that journaling is the first step in handling an emotional wound. Journaling, particularly when combined with full treatment such as therapy, gives us a powerful arsenal, particularly when the pain is so deep, it doesn't seem to go away.

It takes work – hard work – on our part as well as an insatiable desire to heal. When I first began journaling my feelings regarding my father, I wanted only a safe place to express my emotions, but I received much more than I ever expected. I was finally able to release myself from the pain that had once held me captive. This is why I invite you to review them below.

After you read my letters, I hope you will be able to see how self-awareness enabled me to let go of my past wounds and heal from the inside out. Furthermore, I encourage you to take note of anything that stood out to you and/or caused you to relate to my past feelings of pain and shame in regard to my father's absence.

And now, here are some of the letters:

Letter 1: *"My memories of you"*

November 1, 2006

Dear Father,

I have been thinking about writing these letters to you for several years now. There are so many things I need to say to you, so many things I want you to know, and so many questions to ask.

I wanted to get these letters to you in order to share with you what life has been like in your absence. While writing, I realized I have yet to receive an unexpected phone call, a surprise let-

ter, or maybe a birthday card. I entertained hopes of such things, when in fact, I should have known better. How could I forget how easily you seemed to ignore my existence?

I have very few memories of you. However, the saddest memory I have of you is when my late grandmother got my sister and me nicely dressed to take pictures at a photo studio in Haiti. You promised you would meet us there; nonetheless, YOU NEVER CAME. The day started out as a beautiful sunny day, a great day. The sky was blue, the air was crisp, and the sun was shining gloriously.

I remember hearing the birds chirping their songs, mirroring the happy song I felt in my heart that day, knowing I was going to see you.

Everything felt perfect about that day, almost too good to be true. And sure enough, it was because you never came to see us. At that moment, I remember feeling as if the clouds had quickly swept across the skies. The sun was no longer visible. The day became dark and melancholy, reflecting exactly what I was feeling inside.

I must have been about five years old at the time. And although I was very young, I remember feeling very sad and very upset. I remember everything about that day, Father.

Vladimire Calixte is the older child at age 5, sitting alongside her little sister.

What stood out was the fact that you never came. I just simply couldn't understand it! What was I to you, anyway? Was I a mistake you wanted to deny?

And from that moment on, I started to internalize your absence. Wow, I gave you so much power!

Can you relate to this letter? Do you remember a time in your life when you felt this way? What happened? Looking back, what would you have said to your younger self?

_____

_____

_____

_____

_____

_____

Letter 2: *"What life was like without you."*

November 2, 2006

Dear Father,

In the past, "Father" would bring up feelings of pain, lonely nights, and years of questioning why I wasn't good enough for you. When I thought of you, the only feelings that came up were frustration, hurt, anger, loneliness, resentment, and bitterness.

I felt these emotions in silence for years. None of my friends have ever heard me speak of you, and when they did ask me about you, it would conjure up all kinds of negative feelings – hurt, diminishment, and blatant disrespect!

People like to say you can't miss something you've never had, but I beg to differ. I never had you in my life, but I missed you. I missed you when I learned how to talk; I never called anyone "Daddy."

Unequivocally, that is the word I have used the least since I learned to speak. I missed you when I learned how to ride a bike; my mom taught me how. I especially missed you when I saw a father and daughter interaction somewhere. I would see a young girl walking with someone who looked like her father and would say to myself, "I missed that."

I missed you when I earned straight As on my report card. I missed you when I graduated elementary, junior high, high school, and college.

I missed you when I went on my first date. I missed you when I got engaged. I missed you on my wedding day—you walking me down the aisle and our father-daughter dance.

I missed you a million times as I grew up, and oddly, some of them I didn't realize until I got older. Was it the same for you? Did you miss not being there for me? I can't even count the number of times I've cried myself to sleep, wondering why you did not wish to see me or speak to me. I never understood it!

I can remember days when I felt down and had no idea why. I was engulfed in a sense of emptiness I could not articulate, and years passed before I understood the source of my anguish: your absence. Living without you tormented me for a long time.

I don't know what hurt more—the fact that you were not there, or your lack of interest and involvement in my life. I deeply yearned for your love, validation, and acceptance. I wanted to feel that my existence mattered to you.

The growing realization that I was invisible to you started to eat away at my very being. I was starving for you, Father! Looking back, I was fragmented and broken, as so much of my identity was defined by your absence. Wow, I gave you so much power!

Letter 3: *"Feeling robbed of my 'girlhood'"*

November 3, 2006

Dear Father,

I was supposed to be your "little girl." I needed you to tell me how pretty I was and later, I needed you to be the first man to tell me I was smart and beautiful. I needed you to be there to talk to me about boys. I needed you to hug me and tell me how proud you were of me, as I was not a bad girl. When I was in high school, I needed you.

I needed you to remind me that I could do anything. I needed you to tell me how precious and valuable I was. When I came home in tears and cried for hours after having a bad day, I needed you to be there to comfort me and put your arms around me.

The last time I saw you and hugged you, I was … I actually cannot remember the last time I saw you or the last time you hugged me. I thank God for my mom, as she did the very best she could, but I still needed you.

I needed you during my engagement, my wedding, and when I had thirty-two fibroids removed. I needed you to care.

But you did not care. I needed you to know me. My pain ran deep, and as much as I have tried to deny it or silently "deal with it," your absence brought much grief into my life. What would you have lost by being in my life anyway?

I felt cheated and robbed of my "girlhood" without you. However, as the years went by, it became painfully obvious that I did not exist in your eyes. Wow, I gave you so much power!

Letter 4: *"Engulfed in flames"*

November 4, 2006

Dear Father,

I needed you when our apartment caught on fire. On a very cold January day at age fourteen, I watched as our apartment was engulfed in flames. As the fire screamed, I couldn't help releasing a loud screech of my own. In horror, I watched as the enormous orange, angry flames quickly and savagely wiped out everything.

Our apartment was completely destroyed by the fire. All I can remember is my sister, cousins, and I dashing outside into the cold with nothing but the clothes on our backs. I remember hearing the alarming moans of the approaching sirens as they announced their urgent business to all within their range.

As the attention-grabbing sounds of whistles, bangs, gearshifts, and bells of the fire truck and the undulating wailing of police trooper's sirens got closer, I remember how my stomach quivered in utter disbelief and shock.

Our apartment had reached the critical point, and the crest of the burning residue melded into a bigger blazing inferno. It was a horrific scene to witness! All of our apartment's memories were burning right before our very eyes. And then, in a flash, the fire vanished. What was left of our apartment was an unnerving sight.

I will never forget the look on my mom's face. She was at work when the fire started. Not wanting to alarm her too much, the authorities informed her that she needed to go home due to an emergency. To me, it was as if her body didn't know how to react to what was left of our apartment.

Her face went slack, her mouth was slightly open, her body was unmoving, and the color drained from her face as she stared wide-eyed at something no one else could see. She froze up to a point at which I could hardly see her breathing.

She let out a sudden sigh, and opened her mouth as though to speak. However, nothing came out. With each of us by her side, she stood there with tears in her eyes, her face consumed with fear.

We spent the night with one of my mom's very close friends. I remember praying for the night to last a lot longer, because when the dawn brought about a new day, we would be left with the big question: "What do we do now?"

Where were you, Father? Where were you when we so badly needed to be comforted as a result of losing everything? Wow, I gave you so much power!

Letter 5: *"Masking my pain"*

November 5, 2006

Dear Father,

For many years, I let your absence define me silently. I was angry with you and desperate for your approval. I NEVER felt I was good enough, because I was looking for the approval and recognition I needed from you.

I spent years of my life living with regrets and trying to be perfect. I started to live my life around what people said and thought about me. For a very long time, almost every decision I made was centered on trying to please and meet everyone else's expectations.

Everything I did was done to please others! I was a chronic people-pleaser. I was never fully present, as I was consumed with pleasing "them." I would extend myself emotionally and financially, even when I didn't have the resources to give.

Since you had rejected me, I felt a constant and insatiable need to be accepted and approved by others. What's worse is that I didn't have a clue as to who I really was, since I spent most of my life doing and being what others wanted or expected from me. Criticisms made me cringe, because they meant I was not perfect! When a fault of mine was exposed, I felt that my "perfectness" was threatened, which made me defensive and un-happy.

I remember ruminating on criticisms and reading into them much more than the person had intended. I was never really happy, because I viewed everything through the prism of my own insecurities.

In my mind, criticisms gave legitimacy to the reason why you were not in my life. I realized I was afraid of making mistakes and failing, because if I made a mistake or if I was not "perfect," it gave some validity to your absence.

Consequently, I made a deliberate decision to hide and bury my feelings of rejection and inadequacy. I also chose to cover my toxic shame by pretending to be perfect. Looking back, I didn't even feel worthy of God's love. I thought if I was not good enough for an earthly father, how could I be worthy of my Heavenly Father's love?

My thinking was so warped when it came to you, because at the time I couldn't even find solace in God. In hindsight, I gave you so much power. I let your absence define my very being.

Letter 6: *"Academia"*

November 6, 2006

Dear Father,

Academia was my escape. School was very easy for me; I loved and enjoyed it. I quickly realized that school provided me with the validation, recognition, and approval I so deeply craved from you, Father.

Although I was in pain inside, academia was one of the ways I masked that pain—the pain of not having a father and wondering why you did not want me. Why didn't you want to get to know me? I had such a low self-esteem. However, I hid these feelings by excelling in school. Wow, I gave you so much power!

Letter 7: *"My voice"*

November 7, 2006

Dear Father,

It was not until my sophomore year of high school in Mr. Ricardo's talent class that I realized I could sing. Imagine my surprise when I sang in front of the entire class and received a standing ovation.

Singing not only became my passion, but like academia, it was another outlet for gaining and feeling accepted—i.e., gaining the acceptance I so deeply yearned for from you. The more I sang, the more compliments I received.

I also came to realize that I was singing my pain away. I sang very often in the church in Brooklyn, where I grew up. Singing back then was one of the ways I escaped my pain—the constant, nagging pain I felt because of your absence.

When it came to academia and singing, I no longer felt invisible. I mattered! However, I felt so conflicted. There I was—my name associated with words like "talented," "most likely to succeed," "gifted," and "intelligent," yet I struggled and questioned my sense of worthiness.

I have spent most of my life trying to be good enough, so that you would finally love me. Although my mom took very good care of my sister and me, the little girl inside wanted desperately to experience your love.

I hungered for your love and involvement. On the surface, it appeared as though I had it all together. However, deep down inside, my heart was broken.

Wow, I gave you so much power!

Letter 8: *"My shopping high"*

November 8, 2006

Dear Father,

I also started shopping my pain away. I was shopping myself out of the hurt I was feeling as a result of having been abandoned by you. Shopping became my emotional harbor where I was able to relieve my frustrations, anger, and distress, or so I thought.

Shopping gave me a powerful, euphoric feeling that quickly became very destructive. It became very addictive. When I was feeling bad and purchased something that looked good, it made me feel better.

Shopping made me forget about my pain at least temporarily, as it provided me with sensations of safety and warmth. Shopping began to fill an enormous void. I was on a quest to "purchase" inner solace and happiness. Ironically, the more I shopped, the less happy I felt. Wow, I gave you so much power!

Letter 9: *"Reality sets in"*

November 9, 2006

Dear Father,

The more I shopped, the more compliments I received. By the time reality began to set in, I had incurred a vast amount of debt. Although today I am no longer addicted to shopping, I am still paying (literally) for that "shopper's high." Wow, I gave you so much power.

When reality set in, I was also overcome with toxic shame. How could I have allowed this to happen? I blamed myself and became fixated on my shortcomings as a result of my shopping binges and the negative financial consequences.

My anger lingered for so long that I started to punish myself. Ironically, this toxic shame became very familiar and, therefore, felt safe. Your absence left me with emotional wounds so deep that they manifested in destructive behaviors (addiction to shopping and people-pleasing).

I reacted and attempted to resist this toxic shame by looking for the approval and acceptance of others.

Oh God, I was in such deep pain. I gave you so much power!

Letter 10: *"My mom did her best"*

November 10, 2006

Dear Father,

My mom did the very best she could as a single mom of two. Upon migrating to the States, she worked very hard as a nurse's assistant for several years. She was the sole provider, sending money for my sisterand me back home in Haiti.

Eventually, she attended school to become a licensed practical nurse. Today, she is an incredible nurse. Should the truth be told, I did not appreciate her before, because I was too busy being angry with you. You were not around, and it was easier for me to take it out on her. For years, I directed all of the anger and pain I felt towards you at my mom.

I was really angry with you. I was so infuriated that I could not see all of the good my mom did. Mom, I am so sorry! Please forgive me. You are a phenomenal woman. Everything I am to-day is because of you.

Mom, I know that you, too, internalized our father's absence, but you were not to blame. Thus, I hope you find the courage to forgive yourself.

Wow, Father! We all gave you so much power!

Letter 11: *"I don't even know you."*

November 11, 2006

Dear Father,

I have had time to sit and reflect on what hurt me the most about our relationship as "Father and Daughter." The truth is, we do not have a relationship. I don't even know you! I don't know your favorite color, your favorite food, etc. The only thing I do know is that you gave me life.

My sister and I have attempted on numerous occasions to reach out to you, but you have not responded. It's been so many years since I saw you or even heard your voice. Frankly, I have forgotten what you sound like. Would you recognize me if I were to pass you on the street? Wow! It's as though we are complete strangers.

I do remember that you and I look alike. My mom has expressed on numerous occasions how we look so much alike that even our eyebrows are the same. Isn't that something?

I wonder if that was the reason why for a long time, I did not like what I saw in the mirror. Oh God! It hurt so much back then with all that self-loathing.

Wow, I gave you so much power!

Letter 12: *"The man of my dreams"*

November 12, 2006

Dear Father,

The anger I felt towards you started to dissipate once I met Benjamin. We have been married for two years now. You were the first man to break my heart, and Benjamin was able to mend it.

The most difficult part of our relationship was accepting that I was worthy of his love. For so long, I was plagued with low self-worth and felt unlovable. I had never known the feeling of being completely loved and protected by a man until I met Benjamin.

Because of Benjamin, I now know what love isn't. You see, Father, love accepts, values, approves, validates, and protects. Benjamin takes very good care of my heart. He is a constant reminder that GOD heard my prayers and did not forget about me.

Benjamin is a wonderful husband and will be a great father some day. I am truly blessed to have him in my life. One of my greatest joys is to know that my future children will NEVER have to write letters of this sort. They will know and understand the value of a complete family.

Letter 13: *"From pain to inner peace"*

November 13, 2006

Dear Father,

I am not sure of the exact moment when I began to heal from your absence. About two years ago, I remember waking up one day feeling tired of living with the torment and anguish that had plagued my existence for so many years. I decided to take responsibility for my own life.

Just as darkness cannot exist in the presence of light, blame cannot exist in the presence of responsibility. Emotionally, I paid a huge price as a result of your absence. But no more! I no longer wanted to be a victim. I am an adult now, and I don't need to depend on you for my emotional well-being.

I made a conscious decision to stop allowing your absence to destroy my life. I have decided to take back what is rightfully mine, Father—my inherent right to be happy and fulfilled, and to be my true self.

I can remember a time when I had such self-loathing. When I looked in the mirror, I did not like what I saw. Now, however, when I look in the mirror, I see someone who is imperfect, but whole and free. I would rather be whole than perfect.

I knew I did not want "fatherless daughter" or "Mrs. Perfect" written on my tombstone. They don't describe who I am. I am loving, kind, and passionate. I am no longer afraid; I am living now.

Writing these letters was one of my pathways to healing, as it provided me with a way to cleanse the wounds you had brought into my life.

I had no choice about what you had done (your absence), but I finally had a choice as to how I would remove the aftermath of the pain you had created. That choice gave me power over my own life and feelings, and truly released me from the bondage that was surrounding me.

Today, singing has become a way for me to express my thoughts and feelings. It is one of my constructive outlets. Singing is cathartic for me! It's no longer an avenue to get approval from others, because I now sing out of love.

I further realized that I wanted out of this deep pain. I no longer wanted something that caused me so much pain. I no longer hungered for your love and involvement. Moreover, I know I am good enough, Father. Wow, it feels so good to see that on paper!

I believe my journey from pain to inner peace also began when I started to take notice of my blessings. Gratitude can change our attitude and perspective on everything, no matter how deep and raw our wounds.

Albert Einstein once noted, "I could choose to live my life in two ways: one is as though nothing is a miracle; the other is as though everything is a miracle." I made the conscious decision to see everything as a miracle. I began to acknowledge that although I did not have a daddy, I have been blessed and surrounded by people who love me. Thus, I started to accept and embrace life without you, Father.

I further realized that in all of that lingering anger, I was the only person who was affected. I had to take an honest look at my life and had to start really listening to the still, quiet voice of conscience. Who was all of this anger and resentment really taking a toll on, anyway? Me! It was eating away at me. Who held that anger in her body and mind, you or I? I did! Indeed, as far as you were concerned, I did not even exist.

In my journey from pain to inner serenity, I started to re-claim my life so that I could begin living the life I was meant to live. I now understand that I have to give myself what I had hoped to get from you: love and acceptance.

For the longest time, I thought I was the only one missing out. However, I now understand that it is you who missed out.

You have missed out on so much. You missed out on great-ness. I am born for greatness, Father. It took years for me to say and mean this, and I am worth it.

I no longer need your approval, Father. I forgive you, Father, for all the hurt you have caused in my life, and I am letting it go now, closing this door. I have taken my power back!

Letter 14: *"I forgive you."*

November 14, 2006

Dear Father,

I forgive you! I forgive you because you didn't know better. If you had known better, you would have done better. You did what you felt you had to do.

You made the decision not to be in my life, and now I have made the decision to forgive you.

I am not saying it was easy. Forgiving you was a matter of life or death for me. There is such power in self-talk, and I was able to say to myself, "I am going to exercise a conscious choice to forgive you, because I refuse to be locked in the bondage of hatred and resentment for the rest of my life."

Your absence no longer brings up all the many negative and raw feelings I harbored towards you. Today, I am free! I have taken my power back!

Final Letter: *"I forgive you, Vladimire."*

November 15, 2006

Hi Vladimire,

I feel strange writing to you. I have lived with you for so long, and we have never had a one-on-one, heart-to-heart conversation. I have tried hundreds of times to talk to you, and begged you to listen to me, but you ignored me, told me to wait, criticized me, or told me to be quiet.

Don't get me wrong. I'm not complaining. I just need to say that I forgive you. I love you so much, but it has been hard, so please listen to what I tell you. All I need from you is to listen. You can ask questions if you don't understand something or to help me when I'm stuck, okay?

I forgive you! It feels amazing to say that and to mean it. All the energy it took to hold on to that pain and anger! For years, I searched and sought approval, and in my journey through self-awareness I found self-love, acceptance, and forgiveness.

I allowed my father's absence to bring me to the brink of self-destruction, but no more! I no longer have to feel my stomach churning with dread and uneasiness because of toxic shame. I no longer have to look down or avoid eye contact out of fear I have been "seen" and am therefore being judged.

No more will I grapple with the constant thought of "What will they think?" Not only was this debilitating; it also kept me in bondage. No more performing and pleasing! From now on, just being!

I am truly free, as I no longer view my flaws as rooms behind closed doors I tried to keep locked so that no one could see the contents.

After reviewing my letters, were you able to see how self-awareness enabled me to let go of my past wounds and heal from the inside out? Was there anything that stood out to you as you read the letters—something that caused you to relate to my past feelings of pain and shame with regard to my father's absence, or my present state of self-awareness and freedom?

As a therapist, when a client comes to see me and declares, "I am having empty feelings," I can look into this person's eyes and know exactly what he or she is feeling because I've been there.

In sharing these letters with you, I am:

Allowing you to see how I have struggled through my own fragile moments and survived.

Admitting my own fragility and showing my vulnerability.

Revealing that our minds and hearts are not meant to be controlled, but simply need to be heard.

Finally, these letters truly allowed me to delve inward in order to find the answers I was seeking. We cannot solve a problem we won't confront! Self-awareness changes your language from victim to overcomer. People who are self-aware are not only in tune with their feelings, but are able to relate to their feelings from an objective point of view. For example, instead of saying, "I am angry" or "I am ashamed," self-awareness, says, "I am experiencing shame or anger." When approached this way, anger or shame is not you. It's what's happening to you, and therein lies self-mastery. This approach puts you in a position of personal power, because when anger, shame, or sadness arises, you can do something about it.

To reiterate, if something is *happening to* you rather than *being* you, you can find a resolution. One may now change the question and ask, "If I am feeling angry or frustrated, what is the source of my anger, frustration, or shame, and what can I do to seek the calm?" If you associate a feeling with who you *are*, then it has power over you. However, if a feeling is what's *happening to you*, you have power over it. That is how self-awareness transforms the soul.

Self-awareness awakens your inner strength, thereby putting you in a position of personal power. Instead of being a bystander in your life's journey, you become a willing and active participant.

At the same time, self-awareness also quiets the ego and thereby quells the inner critic. The ego and inner critic are subjective. Self-awareness intentionally and consciously rejects the ego, truly unburdening us from it.

After a tremendous amount of thought, I have come to the conclusion that once we experience a shift in our language as a result of practicing self-awareness, most of us will no longer view ourselves as defective. For someone who has experienced years of abuse, shame, or abandonment of any kind, this can be a powerful revelation! Journaling—which in my own case, involved writing my deepest, most sensitive thoughts and feelings about the internal source of my pain—is a truly remarkable tool to help us get "naked and transparent" in order to become more self-aware. I hope you, too, find it useful.

Chapter 8

Tips on How to Attract Your Ideal Partner after Becoming More Self-Aware

Tip #1:

Know that you are worthy of love. It all starts with self-love.

We often hear some single women complain about the shortage of good men, adding that all of the good ones are already taken. My question to those women is: Who says?

Once you have uttered these words, you have already allowed yourself to become emotionally unavailable, and your words will begin to manifest. Then, when you meet a man, what do you do? You are never fully engaged or present, because you have made the assumption that all of the "good men" are taken. It is important to note that on a deep level, what you are really saying is that you are not worthy of a good man.

Because you do not feel worthy of love, one of two things will happen. You will either come across a really good person but push him or her away, or you will end up attracting someone who is not healthful for you. Either way, you end up unhappy. You cannot perceive what you feel you are not worthy of. If you don't feel worthy of love, then find the source of that feeling. I challenge you to spend some time and do the "soul work" needed in order to uncover the people and situations that contributed to the feelings of unworthiness. Ask yourself: Has someone treated me poorly or led me to feel unworthy of love, happiness, or respect?

_____

_____

_____

_____

_____

_____

_____

_____

_____

_____

_____

_____

_____

_____

_____

_____

For many of us, the deep-rooted conviction that we are not worthy or deserve good things makes us resistant to taking care of ourselves as fully as we should, leaving us stuck in destructive relationships and situations that are not serving us well.

Many of us deal with issues of worth; we feel unworthy of love, success, happiness, etc. If you are struggling with this issue, then you must consciously choose to work through it. Self-awareness is about training ourselves to see the truth. We all know the truth can be very painful and downright grueling. Nevertheless, working on these issues frees us to attract healthy, loving relationships, which is something we all deserve.

Finally, know that you cannot give to others what you do not have for yourself. I have come to understand that genuine love is about showing up day-in and day-out. In a relationship, love is about supporting one another and supporting each other's dreams. It's about sticking together whether there is a raise or a layoff.

How can you possibly extend that authentic love to another person when you have not extended that same love to yourself? Moreover, we have all heard the adage: you have to love yourself before someone else can. If you don't love yourself, then that's the energy you will channel in every area of your life.

The way you can show self-love is by channeling your true self. You can do that by releasing other people's voices from your mind and emotions. Think about it this way: it is imperative that we live in what we want and move towards it. Again, if it's genuine love you want, you must first love yourself and constantly be moving towards self-love. Thus, the amazing shift begins.

At this very moment, do you love yourself for who you are, or for who someone led you to think you are?

_____

_____

_____

_____

_____

_____

_____

_____

_____

_____

_____

_____

Tip # 2:
Check Your Motives

Many of us have been taught to operate from a place of fear or lack and scarcity. What do I mean by that? Let's examine the belief that some single women feel there is a shortage of "good men."

When you are operating or channeling this thought, you get stuck in an unhealthy, unhappy relationship. One may think: I know he doesn't treat me well. Nonetheless, if I leave him, I will be alone. We are always thinking about what we are going to lose.

However, when we train ourselves to see the truth, we begin to let go of situations and relationships that are not serving us well. My question to you is: What will you gain when you say, "I no longer want to be stuck in this abusive relationship?"

Sometimes, the fear of being alone clouds our judgment. As a result, we don't ask the right questions during the incipient stage of meeting someone. Some of the most important questions we fail to ask before getting involved in a committed relationship include:

- Why do you want to be in a committed relationship?
- Have you healed from your past relationships?
- How do you handle anger?

- Do you believe in and practice monogamy?
- What are some of your immediate goals and dreams, and how will you go about accomplishing them?
- What are some of your pet peeves?
- What do you expect to get out of a relationship?
- What do you expect to give in this relationship?
- What makes you happy?
- What are some of your strengths and weaknesses as a mate?
- Do you or did you have any addictions? If so, what were they?

Although many of us are eager to be in a relationship, we often subject ourselves to abuse or attract the wrong partners because we don't take the time to date a person before committing ourselves to him or her. Courtship is so important, because it allows us the opportunity to get to know someone on a truly emotional, mental, and spiritual level.

We are in such a rush to get married and have children due to the fear of being alone that we do not take the time to ask the right questions. What's more, we don't ask enough questions—the hard questions we need to ask before we say, "I do."

Let's use the same example of a single woman who feels there is a shortage of men. Again, when you are operating from a place of scarcity, you tend to hold onto someone or something that is unhealthful for you because you feel that shortage. Then you start making excuses by saying, "He is not that bad." The idea of this "shortage" will cause you to become increasingly resistant to the evidence in front of you, and you will become more and more disconnected to your true core self.

If you are presently in a relationship that is not serving you well, what are you motivated by?

_____

_____

_____

_____

_____

_____

_____

_____

_____

_____

_____

_____

Tip #3:
Get into your life: Know that you are already complete.

We all bring our fears, vulnerabilities, and unrealistic expectations from childhood into our adult relationships. If left unresolved, many of us also bring our hidden issues, such as fear of abandonment, anger, mistrust, and neediness. When we bring all this negative baggage into a relationship, it is unrealistic to expect that other person to complete us (i.e., to resolve all these issues). If you believe you will be complete once you meet Mr. or Ms. Right, I am here to tell you that operating from this mindset can be extremely exhausting and damaging to your happiness and self-worth. When you believe you have found the person who completes you, you will do anything to keep that person, even at the expense of your inner core.

Today, I challenge you to free yourself from the belief that you are incomplete without that man, that woman, that expensive car, and so on. Our self-worth is often tied to having others to love us, and if they don't, we feel empty and alone.

Furthermore, we are so busy searching or waiting for someone to complete us that we never get into our lives. What do I mean by "getting into your life"? It means making a conscious decision to show up in your life. When you get into your life, you will begin to connect with your soul.

In your core, you are not incapable of anything. In your core, you are happy now. In your core, you no longer engage a limited negative past or a worrisome future. When you get into your life, you spend more time enjoying who you really are.

Getting into your life is about consciousness and the choices we make in our lives. When you get into your life, you come to believe the following: "Yes, I do need to lose weight in order to be more healthy. However, I don't need to lose weight to be happy or get a mate." In your core, you become aware that you are complete in every way, and in every situation. Complete the sentence below. I ask you to reflect on what is happening inside of you while you are responding to this question at this very moment.

I feel incomplete without:

_____

_____

_____

_____

_____

_____

_____

_____

_____

_____

_____

_____

_____

_____

Because:

_____

_____

_____

_____

_____

_____

_____

_____

_____

As you examine your answers, I hope you will discover that you are valuable and loved with or without a relationship. There's nothing wrong with desiring to have a mate, but knowing that you are whole without one is the key to achieving personal power.

Tip # 4:
Are you the type of person you want to attract?

We attract what we put out! Think about that. You may say to yourself: "I would like someone who is honest and transparent." Well, are you forthcoming and honest in your relationship, or have you learned to camouflage the traits you deem less desirable?

Are you kind to yourself or harsh to yourself? When you stop abusing yourself with your words and actions, you will stop attracting a man or woman who wants to control, manipulate, or abuse you. To reiterate, you have to live in what you want and move towards that.

The more you work on bettering yourself and raising your level of consciousness, the more likely you are to attract someone who is healthier and more healthful for you. If you are not living from your inner core, you are going to attract someone who mirrors that. We have all been there.

Understanding this concept and applying it to your life really helps you make sense of relationships and move forward positively if you choose to. You will attract what you want in your relationship when you are aligned with the person you are at your core.

Until you choose to do that, you will always experience inner turmoil between your true self and your representative.

And in a relationship filled with authentic love, in order to keep the commitment strong, we must work on ourselves. Real love shows us that if we strive to be our best selves, we can each find a partner who does the same. Honesty takes emotional awareness and a great deal of courage.

When we are honest with others, it encourages them to be more honest with us. Furthermore, we are then more likely not to be asked or pressured to do things we do not want to do. We will also find out quickly who respects our feelings and who does not.

Chapter 9

How Not Knowing Yourself
Is Holding You Back in
Your Relationships

Our relationships with others provide us with many opportunities to learn about ourselves. I have come to understand that when it comes to relationships, our consciousness is everything. Until a person is willing to accept the truth about him/herself, he or she will not have a clear path to change.

If we are more emotionally honest with ourselves, we will get to know our "true selves" on a deeper level. This will help us become more accepting of ourselves and eventually, of others. It will also help us make better choices about how to spend our time and with whom to spend it. Nonetheless, we cannot change what we are not aware of or choose to ignore.

When you are unaware of who you really are, you will not observe what kind of person shows up within you in your relationships. Consider the friends in your life. Do different friends bring out different sides of you? Maybe you're more reserved with one and more boisterous with another.

Perhaps you're patient with some and quarrel with others. Just as a friend can elicit a particular side of you, so can your partner. Consider and answer the following questions:

Does my better self show up when I'm with my partner?

_____

_____

_____

_____

_____

_____

_____

_____

Does my worse self show up when I'm with my partner?

_____

_____

_____

_____

_____

_____

_____

_____

_____

_____

Perhaps it's a combination of both. If so, what situations tend to bring out a particular side of you?

_____

_____

_____

_____

_____

_____

_____

_____

_____

_____

Primarily, do you like yourself in this relationship?

_____

_____

_____

_____

_____

_____

_____

_____

_____

_____

_____

When you don't know who you really are, you become resistant to paying attention to many relationship red flags. Here are some examples of red flags a number of us tend to ignore:

1. You feel isolated in your relationship.

You are kept away from your family, friends, etc. No relationship can thrive in a vacuum. In fact, overly exclusive relationships in which partners don't want to include others are a hallmark characteristic of abusive relationships. No one is there to witness it when your boyfriend is putting you down, treating you poorly, or being disrespectful. Whether it is a friend, a sibling, or another acquaintance, it can be helpful to include a larger community in your relationship for the purposes of safety and balance.

Have you ever met his/her friends or anyone whom he/she considers an acquaintance? The saying that we are the company we keep often rings true. As such, your sense of the other person's social circle is collateral information. Maybe they are phenomenal people, or maybe they sit around and insult people. You won't know until you meet them. Furthermore, if you are constantly kept behind closed doors, it can be another indicator that he/she isn't considering you seriously as a partner.

2. He or she never passed "Communications 101."

Communication is one of the keys to any successful relationship. It's easy in the early stages of dating when there is flirtation, witty banter, and small talk to feel as though your relationship is a walk in the park. However, what happens when there is a communication breakdown? Relationship longevity is not measured by when things are going well, but rather when the strife enters.

Does your mate give you the silent treatment instead of trying to talk through it? Does he/she make passive-aggressive statements such as, "You know, James broke up with his girlfriend because she wasn't spending enough time with him…"? Does he/she make threats like, "You're gonna regret it if you don't tell me right this instant?" At some point, your partner could be entering bully territory or be manipulative in the manner in which he/she communicates.

When you feel that you are constantly walking on egg-shells not to upset or agitate your significant other, that's when you've entered rough waters, and there may be very choppy seas ahead. Furthermore, when you feel he/she is trying to "punish" you or "teach you a lesson," that's pretty much the green light to move on.

3. He or she talks about past relationships in a derogatory manner.

One thing I can pretty much guarantee is that one way or another, history always repeats itself. (For you, too, by the way!) Find out what happened in your partner's past relationships. How does he/she talk about past relational dynamics? Your partner's complaints about an ex may hint at future complaints about you.

4. Pay attention: How does this person "do" life?

What I mean by this is, watch how your partner makes meaning of difficult situations, past and present. Is your partner open to learning and growing? Does he or she take responsibility for past mistakes? How does this person respond to problems and challenges? The answers to these questions will give you important information about how he/she approaches life.

The most dangerous scenario arises if this person generally takes no responsibility for his or her actions. It is never a good sign if one continually sees life's difficulties as outside oneself. A person's behavior is an integral part of who he/she is.

Pay close attention to the responses in certain situations, and notice how you're being treated in your relationship. If you are trying to determine whether you are in a healthy or abusive relationship, ask yourself the following questions:

1. Can I be myself around my partner, or do I feel the need to be someone I'm not?
2. When we argue, am I abused verbally or physically?
3. Does my partner accept responsibility for his/her actions or blame others?
4. Am I getting my needs met in this relationship, or is it one-sided?
5. Does my partner encourage me to grow as a person?
6. Do I feel fear when I am around my partner, or do I feel loved and accepted as I am?
7. Does my partner ask me to do things that make me feel uncomfortable/disrespected?
8. Does my partner have character traits I would like to possess?
9. Does my partner express his/her emotions in a positive way that makes me feel safe?
10. Can I trust my partner to be there for me when I need emotional support, or do I feel alone or abandoned?

If you've answered these questions with complete honesty, read your answers and notice how you feel overall about your relationship. Although no relationship is perfect, see if there are any patterns you need to pay attention to. If you are being abused or disrespected, or if you simply don't feel good about yourself when you are with your partner, you can always make a different choice.

The more self-aware you are, the more you have power to change anything in your life that isn't working for you, including your relationships. If you've read this far, I congratulate you, because you are on your way not only to becoming more self-aware, but also to attracting happy and healthy relationships.

My hope is that you have gained some clarity about who you are and who you are not. If you have the courage to see what you do to sabotage your relationships, you will gain the power to transform your behavior. Here are some key messages I want you to take from this book:

1. Certain issues emerge in our relationships, because we are not "naked and transparent." That is why it is extremely important to know what we are bringing to our relationships from our childhood or past relationships.

2. When I meet with couples for the first session, one of the very first questions I pose is: What did you bring to this relationship from your childhood or past relationships?

3. We all bring our fears, vulnerabilities, emotional wounds, and issues from our past or past relationships to our new relationships. Until these issues are dealt with, they will infect every aspect of a person's life.

4. Emotional wounds or injuries, much like physical wounds, have to be addressed. An untreated wound or bruise can produce a number of negative feelings, including abuse, addiction, anger, anxiety, bitterness, depression, fear, frustration, hatred, hopelessness, insecurity, irritability, rage, resentment, sadness, violence, and worthlessness.

5. We cannot change what we are not aware of.

6. For many of us, it is difficult to be "naked and transparent" in our relationships due to fear of rejection, shame, and ultimately, disconnection.

7. Many of us have learned to camouflage traits we feel or were told are undesirable. The thought that comes to mind is: "If I share what I am going through or a part of me that is not so desirable, will I still be worthy of connection?" Because we fear disconnection, we don't really allow ourselves to be seen. As human beings, we live for connection.

8. I have come to believe that all of us need to be seen and accepted for who we are at our core, and it is a need that plays out, especially in our relationships. Therein lies the internal adversarial conflict between your true self and your representative.

9. I often think of the example of packing and unpacking our bags or luggage for vacation. We pack our bags thinking that we are going to need all of these things; yet, when we get to our destination, we unpack only what we want people to see. The rest is left in the bags or luggage. This is a subconscious construct built to ward off what the self believes it lacks.

10. Self-awareness allows us to pose the following question to ourselves: "Whom am I attracting and why am I attracting this kind of person?"

11. Have you ever felt that you always attract a certain type of person? We all have at one point or another in our lives! The same kinds of people seem to present themselves to us all the time. They may have different faces and different names, but in the end, the same issues always come to the surface.

12. I have come to believe that we attract how we truly feel and what we believe about ourselves. If you don't feel you are worthy of love and respect deep down inside, you will attract someone who treats you as such. Moreover, we attract the parts of ourselves that need to heal. That's why self-awareness is such a powerful thing.

13. We can think about having a strong, loving, emotionally giving partner all day. However, if deep down inside we don't feel that we are strong, loving, and

emotionally giving ourselves, we will attract what our inner self is sending out into the world.

14. Take some time to reflect on the relationships in your life. I am challenging you to ask yourself, "What am I putting out there to attract the same kind of people to me?"

15. When you come to know who you really are, you become aware of who shows up within your relationships. Furthermore, self-awareness allows us to pose the following question to ourselves: "Do I embody or possess the qualities I want to attract in relationships"?

16. Self-awareness allows us to break the cycle by cultivating an atmosphere of understanding without self-judgment. With self-awareness, we can correct what has gone wrong and realize that a conscious relationship is not for the fainthearted.

17. When it comes to relationships, consciousness is key. Self-awareness allows us to be relationship conscious.

18. We must first learn to become more aware of ourselves. To achieve this objective, we need to step outside ourselves and objectively watch ourselves in action.

19. At times, even well intentioned people may unknowingly practice certain behaviors that ultimately undermine their relationships.

20. Pay attention to how you react to things and how your reaction affects all of your relationships. The key is to know and move towards what you actually need.

21. Self-awareness requires reclaiming the lost, repressed parts of ourselves that we were told were undesirable. It also means we must learn more effective coping mechanisms than anger, tears, or withdrawal, which have become habitual for many people. It means reconnecting through honest and transparent conversation. This is not easy, but it works.

22. A conscious, transparent relationship can restore your sense of wholeness and set you on the path to real love.

23. Self-awareness allows us to come full circle as we begin to realize that everything begins with us. When you create a loving and accepting relationship with yourself, it allows you to look deeper into what you truly believe about yourself.

24. Self-awareness enables us to identify the parts we need to tend to and heal. This is not easy, but it can be achieved through acceptance and forgiveness.

25. The relationships in our lives act as mirrors. When we have a loving relationship with ourselves, the reflection will always be the strong, healthy, loving relationship we deserve.

"When you come to know who you really are, it will change the way you live as well as the way you love."

— *Vladimire Calixte*

Chapter 10

The Power of Doing Your Life: Where Do We Go From Here?

When you make the decision to practice self-awareness, you become engaged in "doing your life." By "doing your life," I mean that you are mentally and emotionally present in every situation, and you understand how your actions affect your life and those around you.

Self-awareness may not be as easy to put into practice. However, with hard work, you can journey from pain to inner peace. From there, you will begin to live from within. Many things in life can change us, for good or bad, and these changes cloud self-awareness. Some things that can wreak havoc on our awareness are:

1. ***Our upbringing.*** We are taught to behave a certain way, and were told some things are bad or good. This means we may get stuck in a rut or fail to try new things to see if we really like them.

2. ***The media.*** We're constantly bombarded with images and messages that tell us how to be, and many of them can change our perception of how we think we should act.

3. ***Our friends.*** We choose friends we think we should be like, or we look for approval from them.

4. ***Our society.*** We understand and do what's acceptable in society. Unless we really have a grasp on our self-awareness, any changes will be on the surface and not at the emotional level where they need to be.

Self-awareness allows you to speak, love, and live from your soul; herein lies the power of "doing your life." When you become self-aware, your actions are no longer dictated by fear. Your life will no longer be motivated by fear because you are in a perpetual state of peace.

You become at peace because you are living from within. When you are living from within, you can never be threatened, regardless of what challenges life may bring. Nothing real can ever be threatened. Things, people, and situations will no longer control your life. If you are living from your soul, you will not have internal turmoil.

When you come to know who you really are, it will change how you relate to your past, how you parent, and how you respond to the difficulties life presents, including your love life. Self-awareness changes the way we live and love.

I can remember a time when the pain arising from my father's absence ran so deep that I couldn't see past my agony. Living that experience was a source of hurt and anger for me. I also had feelings of diminishment.

His absence became who I was. However, through self-awareness, I've come to the understanding that he *chose* not to be around, and this prompted my journey from pain to inner peace.

I hope this book has impelled you to take a little time to engage in some self-reflection by wholeheartedly examining what you want, any unmet needs, and your beliefs and values; thus, ultimately revealing who you really are. Furthermore, I hope this book has challenged you to ask yourself the following question: Do I have a problem with self-awareness?

One definite way to determine if you have an issue with self-awareness is to ask yourself whether you feel someone else is always to blame for the circumstances and situations in your life. Below are some warning signs that you may not be self-aware:

Do you say/ask yourself the following questions?

- What's wrong with them?
- They did this to me for no reason.
- Our friendship ended, and I have no idea why.
- Suddenly, he's not talking to me. He must be moody.

Can you relate to any of these signs? If your response is yes, know that it is never too late to begin to practice self-awareness, as self-awareness is a limitless journey.

If you find yourself thinking the aforementioned thoughts, I challenge you to turn the focus back to yourself and see if there was something you did to push someone's buttons, start an argument, or prolong a disagreement.

If someone is upset with you and you feel it's "out of the blue," take a moment and see if perhaps you have been pushing him or her towards anger or resentment for a while. Sometimes subtle nagging or contempt builds. This is a good time to reflect on your own actions.

Self-awareness is the pathway to freeing our souls. Our souls desire to be free from shame, fear, and other issues that are keeping us from living our truth. It is only when we live our own truth that we can attain true personal power. Self-awareness begets truth, and truth begets personal power. What an awesome way to live!

What is your life telling you that your soul needs right now? Is it to be kind to yourself? Is it to show your vulnerability? Have you been harboring so much shame that this shame has become your identity? Whatever your soul is speaking to you at this time, know that peace is attainable. When you make a decision to practice self-awareness, you are saying you no longer want to hide, but to live, thus indeed, becoming naked and transparent.

Chapter 11

Additional Tips for Attracting Your Ideal Relationship

"Bad feelings about another person burn your life, but gratitude will eliminate them."

-Rhonda Byrne, Creator of The Secret

For many of us, relationships conjure up feelings of pain, guilt, shame, and abandonment. Many of us have been hurt, and we don't know how to release the pain from the past. In order to attract what you really want in your relationships, you have to let go of your fears and forgive those you feel have hurt you in any way.

One of the things you can do to free yourself is to make the conscious decision to forgive your ex. I had to do this very thing when I forgave my father for not being in my life, because my pain was not serving me. It may be a very difficult process to forgive your ex-partner, but you're worth it. We must learn not to take things people do personally, and realize people do things out of their own insecurities and fears.

The conscious choice to forgive a person does not mean what the person did to us was okay, but it does mean we will no longer allow it to have control over us. One of the things you can do to forgive someone fully is to focus on the lessons you've learned from your experience. Ask yourself the following questions:

1. What lessons can I take from this experience that will allow me to have better relationships?

2. What did I learn about myself as a result of this experience and what can I do differently next time?

3. What am I truly hurt about the most? What are some positive things I can do to empower myself now?

4. What initial message did I get from this experience? What is a new message I can create that will bring me peace? For example, if a partner left you for someone else, the first message you may have received from that experience was that you weren't good enough to be loved. Instead of carrying that fallacy in your heart, you can create a new message that says, "I am lovable just as I am. My partner left me so that I can attract my ideal mate."

Another thing we can do to attract our ideal partner is to become aware of how we treat ourselves. We say we want someone to treat us well, but many of us mistreat ourselves on a daily basis. We call ourselves "stupid," "ugly," and other disempowering names. We remind ourselves of our past mistakes, and often neglect our mental, emotional, and physical needs. Remember: The Law of Attraction teaches us that "like attracts like." You will draw to you who you really are, not what you say you want.

When you begin to be more loving to yourself, you will attract more loving partners and people who honor you. If you find it difficult to love yourself, you can begin the process by making a list of at least five things you like about yourself and repeat them when you wake up in the morning and before you go to bed. If you can't think of one thing you like about yourself, think about what others have said about you and write it on the list. I challenge you to do this for 30 days, and you'll notice a big difference in your self-esteem.

Another thing you can do to love yourself more is to do things that are good for you, and do them on a consistent basis. What is also equally important is for you to become aware of any self-destructive behaviors that are undermining your self-worth.

As I previously revealed, I once had a shopping addiction that was a source of shame for me. Once I recognized the problem and was able to identify the root of it, I forgave myself and was able to free myself from the self-destructive habit that had held me captive.

Learning to love yourself takes patience and practice, and like self-awareness, is a lifelong process. However, you can achieve it if you work at it each day.

Once we work on forgiveness and self-love, the other thing we need to do to attract the person we want is to know exactly what we desire in a relationship. Develop a list of the top ten most desirable qualities you want in a mate, and a list of qualities you don't want.

The reason it is important to know what you don't want is that you will be aware when it shows up. When it does, make a new choice. Be sure not to settle for something or someone you don't want out of loneliness or fear. We often say we want something, but many of us are not willing to wait for it to manifest. We fill the space with something else we don't really want, and this only causes our desires to be delayed. In order to have what you want, you must make space for it in your life and in your heart, and have faith that you will receive it.

This next section of the book is for those of you who are dealing with profound losses, such as a serious illness or death of a spouse or death of a child. One may wonder: I am self-aware; however, is it possible for me to feel pure joy when I am feeling dead inside? In response, I love the following lines from a poem by Bonnie Mae:

"Everyone needs a soft place to fall.
Where no one judges them or hurts them at all.
Some place where they feel safe and secure.
A place where they can heal and give a cure."

My question to you is:

Where is your soft place to fall? Even in your darkest space, I am encouraging you to find a soft place to fall. Let others in on how you are feeling, tell someone you trust your fears, or reach out to an acquaintance you don't know too well. During your most difficult time, it is about giving and receiving the kind of love that heals yourself and others.

Conclusion

"As you become more clear about who you really are, you'll be better able to decide what is best for you—the first time around."

Oprah Winfrey

As a therapist, I am frequently asked by clients how they can overcome PTSD, sexual abuse, anxiety, low self-esteem, and much more. This book was created to shed light on the fact that through self-awareness, we have the power to heal our own lives, and if we look inside for the answers, we will create a life filled with joy, happiness, love, and peace. Regardless of what issues you are facing, you are not alone, and you can turn your life around.

One of the things we can do to change our present circumstances is to be honest about who we are, where we are in our lives, and how we got there. If you find yourself blaming others for where you are, stop and see the role you played. Once you do that, get clear about what you really want and set daily goals that will help you get there.

In order to get what we truly want, we must also be willing to let go of the thoughts, feelings, beliefs, choices, and actions that no longer serve our best interest and find something better.

I am honored to be a part of your journey! If this book has helped you transform your life, I'd love to hear from you!

E-mail me at **Naked@LifeRebuilding.com**

If you are located in the New York area and would like to receive counseling services or participate in the groups below, please contact us at (646) 461-4215 for more information.

Making Love Last Couples' Group

In this 8-week group, couples will be assisted with a range of issues such as improving communication, intimacy, and parenting in a safe and supportive environment. Join this group if you want to invigorate your relationship.

A Time to Heal Women's Group

There is nothing more liberating and powerful than being with others who share similar stories. This weekly women's group will provide you with the opportunity to share your stories in a safe and supportive environment.

Solution-Focused Relationship Group

This 12-week co-ed group will focus on your capacity to cultivate nurturing, loving relationships. The group addresses issues brought in by group members and helps them work through present and underlying problems.

"It's about giving and receiving the kind of love that heals yourself and your loved ones!"

~*Vladimire Calixte*

www. LifeRebuilding.com
Naked@LifeRebuilding.com

About Vladimire Calixte

Vladimire Calixte is a nationally respected, multiple award-winning expert on mental health, self-esteem, abuse, addiction, and relationships. She works with children, adolescents, women, men, couples, and families.

A celebrity therapist, empowerment coach, author, and transformational speaker, Vladimire Calixte is the founder of Life Rebuilding, located in New York City. Her clients include celebrities, politicians, and professional athletes.

Magazines such as *Heart & Soul* and *Ebony* have featured Vladimire Calixte. She has appeared on CBS Radio and FOX News Radio. More programs include ABC's *Here and Now*, *Hot 97 Street Soldiers* with Lisa Evers; and *Café Mocha* with hip-hop legend MC Lyte, Loni Love (of *The Real*), and Angelique Perrin.

Mrs. Calixte holds a Sociology degree from Hunter College and a master's degree in Applied Psychology from New York University. She is pursuing her PhD in Clinical Psychology. Working in the field for more than a decade, she has helped various clients around the world overcome addiction, depression, anxiety, low self-esteem, trauma, sexual abuse, and PTSD. Mrs. Calixte provides individual, couples, and family therapy. **Naked and Transparent** is for the person silently suffering from rejection, abandonment, abuse, low self-esteem, hurt, pain, or anything at all.

With the award-winning **Naked and Transparent: Six Vital Tools for Knowing Yourself and Attracting Healthy Relationships**, Vladimire is an emerging international expert on personal, spiritual, emotional, and professional growth She helps people excel in their lives by helping them redefine who they are from the inside out.

Vladimire is living proof of the incredible strength of the human spirit. The daughter of a man who fathered 52 children. she migrated from Haiti to the US at the age of 8. At 14 she survived a house fire. Now she loves to write, sing, cook, and dance. She is most proud of being happily married for 12 years, and of being the mother of two wonderful young children.

From victim to overcomer, Vladimire is enjoying a thriving private practice where she is helping others live and love from a place of emotional freedom.

For more information, visit www.LifeRebuilding.com.

Fresh Ink Group

Independent Publisher

Imprint: Fresh Ink Group
Imprint: Push Pull Press

☙

Hardcovers
Softcovers
All Ebook Platforms
Worldwide Distribution

☙

Indie Author Services
Book Development, Editing, Proofing
Graphic/Cover Design
Video/Trailer Production
Website Creation
Social Media Management
Writing Contests
Writers' Blogs
Podcasts

☙

Authors
Editors
Artists
Experts
Professionals

☙

FreshInkGroup.com
Email: info@FreshInkGroup.com
Twitter: @FreshInkGroup
Google+: Fresh Ink Group
Facebook.com/FreshInkGroup
LinkedIn: Fresh Ink Group

Fresh Ink Group

Index

Also by Vladimire Calixte
Excerpt from:

Are you in Love or in Need?
Seven Principles to Loving Soulfully

"Why do I keep attracting the wrong person?" In my therapy practice, this is a common question my clients often ask in our sessions when examining romantic partnerships.

My response to the aforementioned question is to always engage my clients in self-introspection. Why?

Because your romantic partner is your mirror. What this means is that your partner is simply reflecting parts of your own consciousness back to you, giving you an opportunity to really see yourself.

"Relationship is a mirror. Every moment the other reveals you, exposes you. The closer the relationship, the clearer is the mirror." —Rajneesh

The people in our lives are often a mirror for what we feel about ourselves. Because "people come together at their common level of woundedness or their common level of emotional health—which is their common level of self-abandonment or self-love." —Dr. Margaret Paul

waitbutwhy.com

Your relationship with your romantic partner enables you to take the closest, most accurate look at who you really are. Having said that, show me who your partner is and I will tell how you feel about yourself. Why, you ask? The person you choose says whether you are loving from your wounded self, your ego, or from your soul.

When choosing a partner from your wounded self, your ego looks like this cartoon.

Brenda and Steve have been dating exclusively for three months. Brenda feels like she has fallen in love with Steve because she feels complete with him. According to Brenda, Steve is meeting all of her needs. "Steve makes me so happy; he is the perfect guy," exclaims Brenda. Yet, Brenda does not know much about Steve as a person. Her only concern is with how Steve is treating her. Steve calls her every day. Not to mention that their talks are filled with romantic conversations. He sends flowers to her job and plans romantic getaways. In all, Brenda describes Steve as understanding and thoughtful. Brenda is head-over-heels in love and thinks, "This man is definitely my soul mate!"

Brenda is loving and engaging Steve from her wounded self—her ego. It's not so much that Brenda loves Steve, but how Steve loves her. By loving that way, Brenda is hand-ing over to Steve the responsibility for her self-worth and wellbeing. Because Steve is doing a great job of attending to Brenda the way she wants to be attended to, she believes she's "in love." The part of Brenda that is in love is really a child or adolescent who is needy for love because she isn't giving love to herself. We can deduce that there's an emptiness inside of Brenda that she expects Steve to fill because she is not taking responsibility for her own feel-ings of self-worth.

Your wounded self is the part of you that feels incom-plete or flawed. It is the part that makes you question your worth or makes you think you are damaged in some way. Your wounded self is always wondering if you are worth loving.

Let's fast-forward to six months into the relationship and Brenda is starting to notice a shift in the kind of atten-tion she is receiving from Steve. Their romantic conver-sations, both calls and texts, have dwindled. He rarely sends flowers to her job and the romantic getaways have stopped. What's more, Brenda is starting to notice some idiosyncrasies with Steve that bother her. Brenda's ideal-ization of Steve as "perfect" and "her soul mate" is slowly dissipating.

Most likely, Brenda will try her best to "change" Steve. It is Brenda's wounded self who believes "if I can get Steve to change, then I am worth it. I am loveable." What Brenda is doing is attaching her worth to Steve's love. Because of this, Brenda's unconscious behaviors moving forward are her attempts to control getting love instead of engaging in loving herself and sharing her love with Steve.

What can we deduce from Brenda's unconscious behaviors:

Brenda doesn't value herself.

Somewhere along her life journey, Brenda made a choice to not value her own worth. She developed this false belief of being "unworthy" or "unlovable" based on something that was said or done to her in childhood. As such, she hands the responsibility of her sense of worth to a partner who cannot fill this void. No relationship with another human being can ever compensate for secretively believing you are not worthy or you don't deserve it.

How Brenda goes about trying to fill the emptiness inside her will cause her to do one of two things: sabotage her present relationship with Steve or settle for a relationship with Steve where she is treated poorly. This will ultimately match her false beliefs about herself. More-over, because Brenda is looking to Steve to provide her with a sense

Would you marry my needs?

waitbutwhy.com

of inner worth, Steve will most likely be looking for the same thing.

waitbutwhy.com

Brenda's relationship is unhealthy because of the unhealthy relationship she has with herself. Since she has not yet engaged in the consistent, conscious practice of defining her own worth and filling herself with love, she needs Steve to fulfill her and make her feel worthy and lovable. This is why Brenda is "in need" rather than "in love." Instead of loving Steve for who he is, she needs him for what he can provide for her. Thus, this is why she is needing to get love. This lack of inner fullness will likely lead Brenda towards trying to have CONTROL over getting love.

Let's trace back to Brenda's childhood. There's something that makes Brenda doubt her own value.

"The people we are in relationships with are always a mirror, reflecting our own beliefs, and simultaneously we are mirrors, reflecting their beliefs."—Shakti Gawain

www.ingramcontent.com/pod-product-compliance
Lightning Source LLC
Chambersburg PA
CBHW060856280326
41934CB00007B/1074